Kicking Against the Pricks

Kicking Against the Pricks

John Metcalf

(**To kick against the pricks.**
To struggle against fate,
to protest when the odds are
against one. See *Acts* ix.5, and
xxvi.14, where the reference is to
an ox kicking when goaded.)

ECW PRESS

Copyright © 1982 by John Metcalf

Canadian Cataloguing in Publication Data

Metcalf, John, 1938-
   Kicking against the pricks

ISBN 0-920802-39-7

1. Canadian literature (English) — 20th century —
History and criticism — Addresses, essays, lectures.*
2. Authors, Canadian (English) — 20th century —
Addresses, essays, lectures.* I. Title.

PS8071.4M48   C810'.9'0054   C82-094759-8 PR9189.6.M48

The publication of this book was assisted by Block Grants from The
Canada Council and the Ontario Arts Council.

Typesetting by Howarth & Smith; printing and binding by Coach
House Press. The cover illustration is by Jeff Jackson, Fifty Fingers; the
cover design by Paul Hodgson.

Published by ECW PRESS, Stong College, York University, Downsview
Ontario M3J 1P3.

The quotation from Seigfried Sassoon in "Punctuation as Score" is
from *Seigfried's Journey 1916-1920*. Published by Faber and Faber. Used
by permission. The quotation from Ernest Hemingway in "We Are
Honoured This Evening" is from *A Farewell to Arms* by Ernest
Hemingway. Published by Charles Scribner's Sons. Used by
permission.

An abridged form of "Without an 'E' " first appeared in *The Canadian
Forum*. "Communiqué" originally appeared in *Canadian Fiction
Magazine*.

Photographs courtesy of Special Collections, The University of
Calgary.

"I read part of it all the way through."
— Samuel Goldwyn

ALSO BY JOHN METCALF

New Canadian Writing   1969
The Lady Who Sold Furniture   1970
Going Down Slow   1972
The Teeth of My Father   1975
Girl in Gingham   1978
General Ludd   1980
Selected Stories   1982

CONTENTS

This book is for Doug and Jill Rollins

Communiqué
Interview with John Metcalf —
February 16, 1981

GEOFF HANCOCK: We were talking a few moments ago about readership. Do you worry about ideal readers?

JOHN METCALF: No, I don't worry about readers at all. My stuff attracts so few of them. My ideal reader, I suppose, is one who's capable of reading exactly what I've written and responding emotionally exactly as the rhetoric dictates that he should. But I think that the idea of tailoring your matter, or your style, or your vocabulary to some notion of a readership is suicidal. I wish I had _more_ readers, of course. What writer doesn't?

GH: So, you're not in favour of literary writers who write for a mass readership?

JM: Well, it seems axiomatic to me that a mass readership and a literary writer are incompatible. You cannot write well for the mass because the mass can't read. Why do we all fence so much about this? Let them eat Harlequins. But what literary writer _does_ write for a mass readership? W. D. Valgardson claims to. And it shows.

If a good writer happens to sell large numbers of a good book, it's usually an accident or the result of promotion or a hangover from a reputation from a period that's gone now.

Promotion can sell _anything_. There's a fascinating book called _How To Write Dirty Books for Fun and Profit_ which is an account of how a group of _Newsday_ reporters wrote _Naked Came the Stranger_. They each wrote a chapter independently and their stated aim was to write as _badly_ as they could. The book was packaged and promoted on the talk shows by the alleged author and it soon reached the _New York Times_ Best-Seller List. Then the writers broke the news it was a hoax. What happened? It sold even _more_ copies than before. It's depressing. You can't even insult people any more.

But what I meant about a hangover from an earlier reputation — Graham Greene's a good example of what I'm trying to say. *The Honorary Consul* was a fine book but I doubt if all the copies sold were *read*. Think of the numbers of that book that were sold through Book-of-the-Month Club. Thousands of people who forgot to get the don't-want card mailed back in time. How *can* one care about such readers when they're so pathetically passive that they let other people choose for them what they're going to read?

Quite a few writers of Greene's age have said that if they were starting now they wouldn't have a chance in hell of finding the same readership. V. S. Pritchett and H. E. Bates said that in their autobiographies. Certain reputations go on like massive snowballs. But what would happen if *Brighton Rock* appeared today?

The same sort of thing's true of Canada, too. We have writers who live on old reputations but they were never much good to begin with. Surely people don't *read* Morley Callaghan, do they? For pleasure? Surely people don't actually *read* Robertson Davies? They're the sort of books that people own to show they're "cultured". Like having a bust of Beethoven on the piano. And Davies plays up to this audience, of course, by going around looking like a bit-player from a movie on Edward VIII's abdication.

GH: Is it safe to say that you're very pessimistic about the educational system in Canada? Your narrator in *General Ludd* . . .

JM: The narrator in *Ludd* is apoplectic on the subject. And so am I. Who isn't pessimistic, other than "educators"? The quality of education has declined everywhere over the last 50 years as the number to be educated has risen. Amis wrote a pamphlet about university education for the Tories in England — I believe it was called *More Means Worse*. Got him into a lot of trouble. It's interesting how so many comic writers gravitate to the political right. Amis writes about this in a book of essays called *Whatever Happened to Jane Austen?*

GH: Isn't that a contradiction for yourself because you are, in fact, a teacher?

JM: Well, I *was* a teacher. But it's been years now since I've taught regularly and I didn't teach then from a deep and committed love of teaching — or of students — but from economic necessity and the fact that I'm not really fitted to do anything else. I *did* care once but it's difficult to keep on caring when you've grasped that the rewards of the system go to the keeper of the neatest attendance-register. And *good* teaching is boring for the teacher because it demands the honesty of drills and repetition. Flamboyant teaching is usually dishonest.

GH: In *Going Down Slow* and *General Ludd* you manage to criticize both the high schools and the universities, at least in Quebec.

JM: *Not* a difficult feat. Yes, they've formed subject matter simply because I've spent a lot of my professional life as a teacher. It seems to me an interesting subject to write about because education has applied at some time or other to all readers. But the educational systems haven't really been subject matter for me. More backgrounds. *Going Down Slow* is less about school systems than about a love affair which ends in betrayal through compromise. Though I suppose it's the system which forces the compromise.

GH: In fact, in your dramatic scheme, the system becomes the antagonist?

JM: Yes, that's probably true not only with the educational world but with the world in general. And particularly with the world as I experience it in North America. I'm violently in conflict with the dominant nature of North American society and this affords me at varying times great distress and great amusement.

GH: This is what you want to write about in your work?

JM: No, it isn't what I *want* to write about. It's what I've been almost *driven* to write about. One writes about where one lives. I happen to live in Canada. I *have* been writing about Canada from the viewpoint of being an immigrant to this country and I get considerable mileage out of the comic and serious contrasts between Canada and Europe. But it's all emotionally complicated. Canada is my home. Soon, I'll have lived here more than half my life. Yet, at the same time, I'm still something of a stranger. But it's *also* true that I feel even more of a stranger in England. I'm caught between two worlds. And one of them exists only in memory — is maybe even partially invented. It isn't difficult to invent England.

You see, the England of my childhood which I remember so richly is totally gone. *That* world had its links clearly and visibly back into the mists of the English past. The Second World War ended so much. In its aftermath, the past was obliterated. Physically, socially — in every way. And then TV finished the job off.

3

My grandfather was a miner who was working in the pits as a child. Who walked along the galleries to the face to start work. For him to read Dickens was close to reading about something remembered. The worlds were that close. And now the squalid, company-owned slum he lived in is razed and the ground is covered with a rash of identical centrally heated bungalows. I couldn't even find where he used to live when I went back a few years ago.

But this idea of not feeling at home. Of being a displaced person. I think a lot of people feel that in Canada. So many of us here are immigrants. Many people *born* in Canada are not really, permanently *at home*. And maybe that's because what we *have* created, or had foisted on us, is in many ways appalling. So I'm driven to attack our failure to create.

Here's an anecdote that suggests something of what I'm trying to say. On my first day in Canada I was walking along St. Catherine Street in Montreal. Gawking. Cops with guns and paunches and wearing shades. Drugstores — just like in Raymond Chandler. Huge buildings. Cars the length of ocean-liners. Everything terrifyingly *American*, right? Then I heard sirens. Two cops on motor-cycles stopping traffic. People beginning to line the sidewalks. Obviously a murder had been committed. And then I heard bagpipes. A parade approaching. Highlanders, for God's sake, in kilts and plaids. The Black Watch. And they were playing what *sounded* like "The Retreat from Gibraltar". And as they passed — and I confess to my heart being moved — I saw that one of the pipers was *black*.

Do you see what I'm getting at? We haven't created a *home*. Our hearts and aspirations are often elsewhere. We live, at least partially, inside other people's dreams.

This constitution business makes me feel *so* ashamed. Trudeau was so right when he said we were more interested in haggling about the price of fish. The Algerians, for example, died in their thousands to create a country. Died under torture. Our constitution — like nearly everything in Canada — is going to be reduced to a sordid business deal worked out by the Head Carpetbaggers. So sad.

GH: Is it because of that nostalgic sense that you tend to draw upon traditional values in approaching your work?

JM: Yes, I suppose I delude myself that there *are* values extant.

4

And in literary terms, one writes against a background and tradition. No literary work is created in a vacuum. The tradition of Canadian writing, in so far as there is one, is largely British — with certain American interminglings. And it's against this past that one looks at the present.

But the problems in looking at North American society are overwhelming. In England, the past is still sufficiently there to form a background against which to examine change. In North America, it's change that is the constant. How *does* one attack the vulgarity of life here? I find it nearly impossible to invent satire because while the ink's still wet actuality has capped whatever grotesqueries you can imagine.

Philip Roth wrote *Our Gang*, a book I'm very fond of, *before* Watergate. It seemed inspired lunacy. *After* Watergate, it seemed closer to a measured account of events.

The difficulties of invention seem to impinge on me every day. Not long ago I was browsing through the mags in a convenience store and saw an article in a Tits magazine that left me shaken. The article was entitled "Anal Drug Abuse".

I've been brooding about that.

What in Christ's name *is* normal anymore?

GH: When you talk about invention, you're also critical of literary invention, the so-called post-modernism . . .

JM: Well, I've never really grasped what post-modernism *is*. I think it was Evelyn Waugh who said that James Joyce went mad to please the Americans. I wouldn't go *that* far but there's an English critic, Graham Hough, who wrote an entertaining essay, saying roughly, as I remember, how embarrassing it would be to have to explain to an intelligent Martian the principles of construction underlying *The Waste Land*.

Hugh Hood and I adopt something of a stance about the Modern to entertain ourselves. As did Waugh, of course. But it's not all in jest. I don't think the "representational", if I can say that, is played out. Think of Richard Yates's stories. I don't *like* reading all that George Bowering stuff. Although my primary loyalties are to style, I like the artifice and rhetoric to connect me to a real world, actual or imagined. The sort of stuff that George is always nattering on about — reflexive fiction or whatever they call it — is like a sort of literary Rubik's Cube.

GH: Which writers are you attracted to?

JM: That's a difficult question to answer because I'm attracted to so many. My favourite writer is probably Waugh. P. G. Wodehouse is one of the century's greatest prose stylists and I delight in his work. Anthony Powell. And then I'm very fond of Keith Waterhouse and Beryl Bainbridge. Kingsley Amis still turns in comic performances from time to time that are cripplingly funny — I'm thinking of the crucial conversation at the end of *Jake's Thing* which is drowned out by a jet plane. I keep returning to comic writing, don't I? It's my real love, I suppose. Beryl Bainbridge even managed a comic rape scene in *Injury Time*. A wonderful writer. The woman feels sorry for the desperation of the man raping her and offers to pull up her sweater so he can feel her breasts and the rapist says, "I can't abide tits". I'd love to have written that. But it's Waugh, I think, who formed whatever grasp I have of the possibilities of the language. Waugh and the poets, of course.

When he was being interviewed for *The Paris Review*, he said something which is central to what I feel, too, about writing. Let me read you this.

'I think that your questions are dealing too much with the creation of character and not enough with the technique of writing. I regard writing not as investigation of character but as an exercise in the use of language. And with this I am obsessed. It is drama, speech, and events that interest me.'

Now, that sentence, 'I regard writing not as investigation of character but as an exercise in the use of language' is a statement that many today would have difficulty understanding. They're so used to the idea of literature being *about* something or of using literature as something else — as sociology, history, psychology, what have you. The idea that it's a verbal structure in the sense in which a lyric poem, for example, is a verbal structure, is an idea that's largely foreign now to most readers of novels — even intelligent readers of novels.

What a work is *about*, its "ideas" — these are the givens, as it were. Any moron can tell you what a Waugh novel is 'about'. Unimportant. What *is* important is how the work is *performed*.

I'm beginning to bore myself.

GH: What did you learn from Evelyn Waugh? Did you learn form, did you learn structure? Did you learn the difference between the novel, the novella, the story?

JM: No, no, nothing like that. I heard a voice and I saw a tremendous craftsman manipulating words in a delicious order. I was offered an example of something damn close to perfection. I suppose I learned a great deal about timing and pacing, about precision and crispness. You couldn't learn anything from Waugh about short stories — and they're really my central interest, I suppose — those and novellas — because he didn't write many stories and those he did write were shockingly bad.

Strange how few good comic stories there are. I can only think of a handful — W. W. Jacobs, H. E. Bates, Kipling, Naipaul — I think Naipaul's "The Night Watchman's Occurrence Book" is the funniest short story in English — no, I can't think of any more. I suppose it's because comic stuff depends too heavily on plot for modern taste. But if I ever manage to marry Waugh's crispness to some of the comic stories I want to write . . .

He's so difficult to talk about. In that same *Paris Review* interview he was asked what he felt about criticism and he said,

"Naturally I abhor the Cambridge movement of criticism" (by which he meant F. R. Leavis and the Scrutineers) "with its horror of elegance and its members mutually encouraging uncouth writing."

Now I'd like to expand on that because I consider my own work to be fairly elegant and it's something I've suffered for at the hands of readers and critics. Critics in Canada don't have a horror of elegance. They don't even know it's there. There's been very little worthwhile critical writing on Waugh. What is there to *say* about a Waugh novel? You see, Leavis and all those lugubrious people who thought D. H. Lawrence was hot stuff somehow managed to ignore the fact that he was clumsy, laborious, repetitive, and unsubtle. He was an obsessive *ideas* man. Evelyn Waugh doesn't really *have* ideas. I don't think many good British writers do. But he turned in wonderful verbal performances of supreme elegance. Now, if you're blind to elegance, what can you say about him?

You can't *explain* elegance. It's pointless to try. It'd be like telling a joke to Rudy Wiebe.

Waugh is one of those writers who will never get extensive critical attention because what exegesis can address itself to the wonder and crispness of the way he uses the semi-colon? Same's true of Wodehouse. You either understand his performance or you don't. And if you don't, then he's a grumpy, cantankerous, drunken old Catholic and you can't see what all the fuss is about. Which is, of course, your loss.

GH: Exactly. You're something like your character Jim Wells in that you're also inside and outside the system at the same time. In *General Ludd*, Wells as a writer is inside the system yet harshly critical of it.

JM: Personally, I'm very much outside the system. I cannot conceive of anything more horrible than being inside. I make raids into enemy territory every now and then when funds are running low. But I don't really think that the people who employ me pretend that I'm massively *with* them.

GH: Does that also apply to where you stand in Canadian literature? Waugh's comment about Leavis and the Cambridge school of criticism might also apply to critics in Canada. CanLitCrit tends to deal with the *ideas* of a fiction and not usually with the technical accomplishment.

JM: Well. Let's take that in two parts. I don't think I stand *anywhere* in the CanLit Scheme. I haven't got a Garrison Mentality and I'm not at Stage Three or a Victim or on Cloud Nine or whatever the fuck all that twaddle was about. My work suffers from a paucity of Indians and Myth. I have very few readers and the critics are still largely baying at the thematic moon. I just potter about making Ronald Firbank noises.

On the other hand, I *do* have *two* entries in the *Supplement to the Oxford Companion to Canadian History and Literature* — one under Metcalf and the other under Metcalfe. I suppose that's *some* sort of distinction.

Now as to critics and their horror of elegance and their mutually encouraging uncouth writing. Says it all, doesn't it? All the criticism we've had in the last ten years has been intellectually embarrassing. Patricia Morley, John Moss, Clara Thomas — I'd rather read Eddie A. Guest *and* fail my Wasserman Test. Our newspaper reviews are not unusually illiterate. And our Literary Establishment has chosen to honour *Bear* and chosen not to honour Hugh Hood, Clark Blaise, or Mavis Gallant.

When people at parties ask me what I do, I'm tempted to mumble, "Pulp-related industries".

GH: Are you trying to improve the standards of writing in the country through *Best Canadian Stories*, through the anthologies that you've edited? You've done something unique in some of your anthologies. You ask the authors to contribute an essay on their stories. Is that part of upgrading the standards?

JM: Let me deal with *Best Canadian Stories* first. That was, in the beginning, just a job that I fell into. But when I persuaded Michael Macklem of *Oberon* to change the title to *Best*, it was a conscious decision to attempt to improve standards. I wanted to produce a book that would be an annual showcase of fine writing — writing for which one wouldn't have to mumble and apologize. A book one could show to an American, an Englishman, or an Australian, without feeling excessive shame.

You've got to consider the *background* of this book. It came out of a literary world which considered Hugh Garner a pretty good story writer. Need I say more? The book isn't really a source of ego-gratification for me. I knew I needed help, needed other literary sensibilities involved. I co-opted first Clark Blaise and then Leon Rooke. Every year I want to quit. It's exhausting. But I realize every year that the book is doing an immensely valuable job. And writers do look at it. Especially younger writers. I hope it gives them something homegrown as a standard. The critics aren't too keen on the book, those that condescend to notice it at all. I suppose it gets a brief review in *Canadian Literature* — I can't remember. It *ought* to get extensive review, of course, because it's among the most important books of any given year. But try telling that to *Saturday Night* or *Maclean's*. It ought to appear automatically as a paperback just as the *Best American* book does but I don't suppose it ever will.

Sales are disappointing. Even after all these years, it still only sells 2000 copies. Some years, less. Some years I'm tempted to throw in the towel but dealing with indifference is part of *being* a writer here.

The quality varies because we're dependent on what writers have produced. Some years are vintage while others are not. But the way the big guns ignore the book pisses me off. When Elizabeth Spencer's *Collected Stories* came out, Toronto went into a tizzy "discovering" her. One big gun Toronto critic singled out a Montreal story "I, Maureen" for especial praise and bemoaned the fact that this fine writer had lived in our midst unknown for the last twenty years etc. etc. But if he'd looked at the acknowledgements page, he'd have seen that he could have "discovered" Elizabeth Spencer's "I, Maureen" years before in *Best Canadian Stories*.

Same's true of lots of other writers. Jack Hodgins, Leon Rooke, Audrey Thomas — and lots of new talent — Linda Svendsen, Keath Fraser, Guy Vanderhaeghe. And we've kept Norman Levine, Alice Munro, Clark Blaise, Mavis Gallant, Hugh Hood etc. etc. firmly in the eyes of what public there is.

All 2000 of them.

I'd have to admit that I'm proud of that book. It's not perfect and we make mistakes. But it's getting better and tougher every year. Look back 14 years and see how far we've come. I confidently expect my Order of Canada any day now. With bar.

GH: And what about the anthologies?

JM: Well, the anthologies grew out of my career as a teacher — out of my reaction to the way Canada was in the early sixties. The first book I did for kids was *Sixteen by Twelve* — I guess I must have put that together in '68 or '69. And at that time there wasn't another even vaguely contemporary gathering of Canadian stories on the market for schools. Incredible, isn't it?

Of course, you have different standards for school texts than you do for trade books. You have to have. To get onto Circular 14, the "approved" list in Ontario, the book has to pass scrutiny by a committee of educational ninnies who check it out for moral purity, sex-role stereotyping, imperial as opposed to metric references, etc. I've included stories in texts which sure as hell wouldn't receive my *personal* imprimatur simply because they might be good stories *for kids*. Sometimes there's no point in casting pearls before gum-snappers. But it'd be nice to be free of the Mrs. Grundies and do a real balls-out book for kids. But again, you don't sell the book to the kid. You sell it to the teacher. And their taste moves like a glacier.

I was *amazed*, you see, when I first came here that Canadians didn't teach Canadian writing. Writers were unknown. Entirely so. So when I did *Sixteen by Twelve*, I asked the writers to write a commentary. I didn't care too much what it was — I just wanted the impact of personality. Then I put in photos, too. It was all a come-on, something to seduce students into reading what they should have been reading — their own literature. It was missionary work.

GH: Was the Montreal Storytellers group part of this missionary work as well? The group you had with Ray Smith, Ray Fraser, Hugh Hood, and Clark Blaise?

JM: Oh, very much so. Hugh Hood and I got that going in 1970. We read in the schools week after week, talked to kids, answered questions for hours, propagandized. We were trying to attract a new generation of readers and we were pushing the idea of a Canadian literature. We wanted to make their own city real to them, show them that Montreal could be imagined just as London is or New York is. We tried to make the *idea* of literature attractive. We were *there* — we weren't just names on a page. As Clark used to say, you can look us up in the phone book.

But we failed. I don't think the literary situation has changed very much to this day.

GH: Yet more than a decade has passed . . .

JM: Yes. It's a long time. And sod-all has changed. Well, here's an illuminating anecdote. A couple of years ago I thought it would be a good idea to do a companion volume to *Sixteen by Twelve*. A book that would feature writers who'd become well-known over the last ten years — obvious names — Audrey Thomas, Jack Hodgins, Kent Thompson, Clark Blaise, Alistair MacLeod, Valgardson etc. etc. Exactly same format as *Sixteen by Twelve* but a new title — *Stories Plus*. Everyone wanted to get away from *Sixteen by Twelve* because it had reduced *McGraw-Hill* over the years to something like a lumberyard. Orders pouring in for 2 x 4 and 3 x 6 and ten sheets of old black joe. Anyway, the book came out and didn't sell. And hasn't sold. You know publishers put cards in complimentary copies of books asking for comments? Every card returned said exactly the same thing — *that they'd never heard of a single one of the writers.*

But you wouldn't need *that* to know we've failed. What other country unloads its literature for half price plus a failed lottery ticket?

GH: Yet one would think that if *Sixteen by Twelve* was going to sell for another 20 years that your work would be read as a result of it.

JM: No. Schools and universities are a captive audience. And, boy, do they long to be free! They do CanLit and secure the credit and then revert with relief to TV. There's no carry-over. CanLit's an artificial thing and it has no real connection with

Canada, with people. The problem isn't so much that people don't read Canadian books — it's that they don't read books, period.

As far as the schools are concerned, what they *should* be doing is basing their literature teaching almost exclusively on Canadian work. If they wanted to teach say, lyric poetry, the basic ideas could be taught using Canadian poems. Same with stories. That's not to argue for the exclusion of anything, you understand. But there's no reason why one shouldn't approach the lyric poetry of, say, Keats, *via* the lyric poetry of Purdy or Nowlan. It's inconceivable to me that you can have a large, powerful, allegedly civilized country which teaches the literatures of two other countries rather than its own. I just find that mind-boggling.

But there's no point in imposing CanLit by legislation. It must come because people want it, otherwise it's as pointless as Consumer Ed. But they'll never want. My small children still bring home mimeographed outline pictures they've coloured in for Thanksgiving with Pilgrims and Turkeys and Red Indians. And my oldest boy's literature assignments are usually to watch TV programmes and report on their wonders.

Dukes of Hazard, man. Brrrm! Brmmm!

GH: Is it one of the intentions behind *Best Canadian Stories* that it might be used as an educational tool? Or is it intended as an accurate commentary on our time?

JM: Well, the educational tools would never use it. It'd involve them in effort and thought. And, anyway, they're still finetuning their responses to Isabella Valancy Crawford. No. That book is charting where we are now. And where we're going. It's a book for readers and a book for writers. In thirty years some academic will mumble it over and declare it to be of seminal something or other. Just as they will with *Canadian Fiction Magazine*. But buggered if they'll buy a subscription, Geoff. There are some wonderful exceptions but in the main they're a sorry bunch.

GH: Has anything changed in the short story in Canada in the past decade? What's happening to the story?

JM: It's changed out of recognition. *Best Canadian Stories* has something to do with that but only in the sense that it's *pushed* the best and served as a showcase. The real credit, obviously, is to the individual writers. It's during this decade that we've seen superb work from Alice Munro, Hugh Hood, Norman Levine, Clark Blaise, Leon Rooke, Mavis Gallant — and there are others. The main advance has been in style and technique and form — all the things that add up to sophistication. We now have *sophisticated* writers who make considerable demands on readers.

Compare this with what we had before. When I arrived in Canada in 1962, the Canadian story was more tale or yarn. I *hate* that word. Tales about lumberjacks and prairie farms. Heavy on plot and light on brains, style, and elegance. Here's a potpourri that suggests what the story was not long ago.

Hugh Garner's uncouthness both literary and moral. He wrote an introduction to Alice Munro's first book. See how closely things overlap? Callaghan's sentimental, ill-written tales. He was never able to leave the reader alone. He typically draws a sketch and then explains what it means. I think of Sinclair Ross stories like "The Painted Door" and "One's a Heifer" — pure hokum — the literary equivalents of the villain binding the maiden to the railroad tracks. Though his big novel's a different matter. I think of Mitchell's *Jake and the Kid*. Of Greg Clark. Of the Leacock Award for Humour.

I know why Levine and Richler fled.

All these writers seemed to have been immune to any innovation whatsoever. The story in Canada was hayseed and provincial, cut off from what the rest of the world had quickly absorbed. Callaghan may have *known* Hemingway but I can't see any evidence that he learned from him. It was Hugh Hood with *Flying a Red Kite* who signalled that we were joining the rest of the 20th century.

There seemed to be an explosion of talent just before 1970 and it's been burnishing itself ever since. And none of it came out of anything Canadian. How could it? Even Alice Munro who's so identified with Ontario drew on Southern writers to create her vision. If these writers have anything in common it's that they drew nourishment from the best that America — and the rest of the world — had to offer.

Perhaps it's the relationship between writer and reader that's changed most in the last 15 years. The good writers are trusting readers to be able to read. The problem, of course, is that there are so few of them to trust.

And you asked where the story seems to be going?

Well, very briefly, it strikes me that what ten years ago would have been considered "experimental" or a bit whacky is now being absorbed into what you might, laughingly, call the "mainstream". The emphasis has shifted away from "content" and it's settled more on "performance".

GH: Which story writers are doing work of merit?

JM: Well, there are the ones I've already mentioned — they're the major writers of stories. But there are lots of other writers who are doing good work. I think we're just going to have to wait and see who keeps going. See if they produce a second book. A third. It's too early yet to predict who's going to follow that 1970 bunch.

GH: Is it any easier now for the new writer? Why have you initiated the *Impressions* series with *Oberon*?

JM: I was worried about how younger writers were going to make the leap from publication in the mags to publication in book form. It's hard for them now with so few publishers willing to even *look* at story collections. And there's some good young writers coming up — producing stuff so much more sophisticated than the stuff I was hacking out at their age. And we have a responsibility to them.

These *Impressions* books feature the work of three young writers in each volume. This gives them a *slightly* larger audience than *Canadian Fiction Magazine* does and it'll get them reviewed a bit but the main thing it'll give them is that huge psychological boost you get from a *book*. It'll spur them on to write more.

After that, they can take their chances with the rest of us, God help them!

The thing is, Geoff — well, as you know with the magazine — we're all part of a tradition and if we don't show responsibility to the tradition and extend ourselves for younger writers — even if it's a pain in the ass and takes time away from what we *want* to be doing — then the whole damn thing's going to collapse. I'm not being consciously *nice*. It's a job that has to be done.

You know, when Hugh and Clark and Leon and I were starting out, I used to think that we'd become part of the mainstream. I don't think that any more. The mainstream now is much more commercial than it used to be. And for younger writers it's going to be worse. Everything seems to be splintering.

Regional presses — a *disastrous* development. *Great Stories from Saskatoon*. Special interest presses. *Gay Maritime Stories*. Feminist presses.

Which reminds me. I was looking at a thing called *Fireweed — A Feminist Quarterly*. In the Notes on Contributors at the back it said of one lady, "she is currently editing an anthology of first-person poems by people who were molested as children".

Amis'd like that.

And there's no consensus about who's good, bad, or indifferent. I was referred to in a review the other day as "a contemporary master of the short story" — this from a most respected academic in an august journal. But there are other academics — Bill New, for example — who think I write so badly that I shouldn't even be mentioned. And I've been around for more than fifteen years. Think of what this means for beginners. There's nothing defined towards which they can struggle. There's no centre. The tradition's faltering. If it gets much worse, I wouldn't be surprised to see the good ones going into exile again.

GH: In your own work, you comment quite strongly on various aspects of Canadian writing. Do you see yourself as a satirist or moralist?

JM: Certainly there's a satirical bent, even perhaps a moralistic bent in my writing. And I mean moralistic in a bad sense. An element of preaching, I'm afraid — I certainly wouldn't deny that.

GH: I was going to say that *General Ludd* is like a one-man demolition derby. *Private Parts: A Memoir* is almost an allegory with the River Eden, the fall from grace, sermonettes . . .

JM: What a revolting word! But, yes. I don't think *Parts* is moralistic at all. But I wouldn't defend *Ludd* against that charge. *Ludd*'s very much a public book. This comes back to what we were talking about before. Canada drives me into opposition — loving opposition, of course. And opposition does tend to encourage sermonizing and castigation and fulminating like one of the gloomier prophets. Bad for the liver. I'm writing another "public" book at the moment — a collection of essays — but when that's done I'll be returning to the gentle blandishments of fiction.

If one cares about what Canada could become, it's difficult to restrain criticism of what it *is*. Which is a mess. And it's a mess for interlocking reasons. Take our cities as an example. For the most part, they're visual slums. This isn't simply because we have bad architects. It's because those with money have bad taste. They have bad taste, in part, because of our educational system and its dominant values — which reflects our political system. There are many people staggeringly wealthy in Canada but the rich middle class wields no artistic influence as it does in other countries. The rich in Canada are joke-people. As in Newman's books. They use their wealth to build stunningly vulgar houses in Hampstead shaped like pagodas.

Our National Gallery *leaks* and our past is busily rotting in our museums because it would be too expensive to install temperature-control. If the wealthy middle class *cared*, the situation would never have arisen.

It all comes back to our attitudes towards Canada. It's always been a place to which people have come from elsewhere to better themselves — a land of opportunity. The reaction to Canada has always been one of lust and rape. It's been raped over and over by greedy people. Despoiled. And not just by the robber barons. The whole ethos of Canada is one of Take. We've not yet grown to a point where people think of ways to give. It's a place from which people extract — as though it were a vast mine — and all they leave behind is ugly tailings. This attitude seems to permeate every aspect of Canadian life. Big Bucks. Top Dollar. How is it possible *not* to hate that?

GH: Do you see your fiction, then, as an instrument by which this may be changed?

JM: No, I'm not *that* bloody daft. Fiction doesn't work that way. But something I say might touch a heart here or there... I suppose that behind a lot of my fiction there hovers a ghost of somewhere else — Europe, England — where there's a different kind of attitude towards the country, where there's been a much longer tradition of passionate caring for place.

GH: This is very apparent if you place *Girl in Gingham* and *Private Parts* side by side.

JM: Yes. The idea of the divorced person is particularly significant to me for reasons which extend beyond the purely personal. I somehow see divorce as being metaphorical in many ways for life in Canada. Everybody knows what we're divorced *from* — from the land itself, from anything resembling a cohesive society, from a past, from our countries of origin. A classic instance of divorce is Mackenzie King's importing old stones from England to erect a folly. Anything, you see, to avoid dealing with *Canada*. The events in *Girl in Gingham* — CompuMate and all the wounded people — suggest, I hope, more than the literal.

I have a pessimistic view of what we've wrought in Canada, a view not far removed from Levine's conclusion to *Canada Made Me*. That doesn't mean that I have contempt for all the individual lives in Canada but the totality of those lives has not created a society yet. We traded one form of wilderness for another — bush for shopping centres.

It sounds arrogant, I suppose, but I want to add my 5-cents worth in my special field to try and raise the standards of one part of our life here. The standards are so very obvious and cast a strong and *uncomfortable* light. We're so frightened of the idea of excellence — and with damn good reason.

GH: You certainly apply those standards to your work, your stories, the rhythms of the sentences, the words, the relationship of one word to another, even the punctuation has a considerable sense of grace and style.

JM: I hope so. I repeat myself but stories are verbal structures. Everyone is so busy grubbing about to find an unfindable "what" that they pay no attention to the "how" — and it's the "how" that *is* the "what". I'm using these terms because I'm referring to John Ciardi's little book *How Does a Poem Mean?* Every English teacher in the country ought to have a copy. We don't read *King Lear* for its silly, pantomime story. We read it because it's written in words that have been forged into compelling order.

GH: In fact, that's something that you often do in your own work. You use words almost for their own sake. Your stories are just filled with very unusual words, odd words, strange-sounding words, words that send us off to the dictionary.

JM: I certainly hope I *don't* use words for their own sake. I only use words that seem to me entirely appropriate within the context and that produce the rhetorical effect I wish to achieve. I certainly don't put words into my stories which *I* have to find in dictionaries. I operate with the vocabulary of which I'm

17

possessed. If certain words strike people as being odd or peculiar or obscure, then that's their problem and not mine.

But I'm *surprised* you say this. Though Doug Rollins said the same thing, too. *I've* always thought of my writing as lucid and simple.

GH: Perhaps that's part of the pleasures of literature, enjoying the deployment of vocabulary?

JM: Well, certainly. You can't restrict yourself to a diet of what you already know. It'd be like refusing to go to great restaurants because they didn't serve hamburgers.

GH: You also use pieces of words and once carefully examined the code letters in a telegram. Letters themselves have specific weight.

JM: Well the examination of a telegram's code letters was to indicate something of the emotional context of the person doing the examining but, yes, I have a deep and probably neurotic interest in what you might call the *calligraphic* look of words on a page. It's part of writing well. All writers do it to some extent.

GH: In fact, the text and typeface of your pages look almost like John Cage compositions. You've got the bold type, the italic type, upper case, lower case, the sentence fragments, and all kinds of voices and textures moving in and out; there's a counterpoint, almost like music to the ear and certainly to the eye.

JM: Yes, that's deliberate. For example, over the past few years I've been working out a system of double and single quotation marks to indicate differing levels of voice. And my use of paragraphing is to get different weights and emphases — rather than for syntactical purposes. I write and re-write endlessly to get the exact look and feel of what it is I'm saying. I'm very concerned that the voices on the page convey the exact nuances that I want the reader to hear. And I can only get the reader to understand those nuances by a very careful control of punctuation and typographical device. And even by the silence of white paper.

GH: Could you give me recent examples of how your punctuation works? Punctuation as music?

JM: It's difficult to do. I can't be brief. I've written an essay on this called "Punctuation as Score" — maybe I could read a bit of that? But it's not as *music* — it's as *score*.

Consider the opening of my story "Gentle as Flowers Make the Stones".

Fists, teeth clenched, Jim Haine stood naked and shivering staring at the lighted rectangle. He must have slept through the first knocks, the calling. Even the buzzing of the doorbell had made them nervous; he'd had to wad it up with paper days before. The pounding and shouting continued. The male was beginning to dart through the trails between the *Aponogeton crispus* and the blades of the *Echinodorus martii*.

Above the pounding, words: 'pass-key', 'furniture', 'bailiffs'.

Lackey!

Lickspittle!

The female was losing colour rapidly. She'd shaken off the feeding fry and was diving and pancaking through the weed-trails.

Hour after hour he had watched the two fish cleaning one of the blades of a Sword plant, watched their ritual procession, watched the female dotting the pearly eggs in rows up the length of the leaf, the milt-shedding male following; slow, solemn, seeming to move without motion, like carved galleons or bright painted rocking horses.

The first eggs had turned grey, broken down to flocculent slime; the second hatch, despite copper sulphate and the addition of peat extracts, had simply died.

"I know you're in there, Mr. Haine!"

A renewed burst of door-knob rattling.

He had watched the parents fanning the eggs; watched them stand guard. Nightly, during the hatch, he had watched the parents transport the jelly blobs to new hiding places, watched them spitting the blobs onto the underside of leaves to hang glued and wriggling. He had watched the fry become free-swimming, discover the flat sides of their parents, wriggle and feed there from the mucous secretions.

"Tomorrow . . . hands of our lawyers!"

The shouting and vibration stopped too late.

19

The frenzied Discus had turned on the fry, snapping, engulfing, beaking through their brood.

The use of single quotation marks round 'pass-key', 'furniture', and 'bailiffs' where double quotation marks would be considered correct has various effects. First, although they are words spoken *to* Jim Haine, they are not spoken to him directly face to face; a locked door stands between the characters. The "incorrect" use of the single quotation marks suggests this distance. Second, Haine's attention is directed elsewhere and these three words are words his mind picks out from what is presumably a tirade. The words 'picks out' in the preceding sentence are important; were the three words in double quotation marks, they would be given greater weight and prominence on the page and this would weaken the intended effect of lack of attention to the harangue. The question of weight (or sheer blackness on the page, if you will) perhaps verges on calligraphy which is related to my third point. Single marks have the appearance on the page of pincers — as if the heard words have been 'picked out' from a flood of other words with tweezers.

The italicized words *Lackey!* and *Lickspittle!* while certainly fulfilling the allowable function of emphasis also do more. Because they lack quotation marks, they are to be understood as words not spoken aloud. But they *are* spoken inside Jim Haine's head to the man beyond the door. Italic hereby becomes interior speech — words formulated but not uttered. This device is now commonly used and commonly understood and has been for years yet it is not described or acknowledged in any of the standard reference works on punctuation.

With the words in conventional double quotation marks ("I know you're in there, Mr. Haine!") we are not only hearing the words of the man outside the door but we're also being made aware that Haine is hearing them too, that his agonized attention is being drawn from the tank of fish; he realizes that the noise has gone on too long and that the frantic parents will devour the fry. The double marks here contribute to action and to our awareness of Haine's consciousness.

Such a simple combined use of single and double marks, then, helps to establish the consciousness of the character and adds intensity and *drama* to his immobility and concentration. It also does away with having to say that he is rapt or staring fixedly or with great concentration. It also does away with having to say that the voice beyond the door was only half-heard or was muffled etc. etc. These effects could not have been achieved so economically and delicately had the conventions been observed.

Well, that's more than enough. Oh what a noble mind is here o'erthrown, eh? But what I'm aiming at is a finished piece of prose which will manipulate the reader without his being aware of it. I want him to flow along with the nuances of the voices, understanding without having to be told directly *how* to understand.

GH: Rather like a jazz composition.

JM: In a way, I suppose. It's a bit like playing in a small group where voices take off and improvise and where the listener is emotionally caught up into the flow of the solo.

GH: Are you influenced in this by the jazz you listen to? I wondered if the rhythms of jazz do affect your prose. Several of your characters attend jazz concerts. Mostly, though, they end up exposing the concerts for the fraud or disappointment they are.

JM: We have to be very careful with these analogies. Pater, wasn't it? "All art constantly aspires towards the condition of music." *Sounds* good, but I suspect it's blather. The problem is that painting and music don't *mean* anything. Words do. Word as *pure* sound reduces you to Gertrude Stein or Edith Sitwell or bad Swinburne. *Not* to be recommended. I *could* say that my writing has been deeply influenced by the paintings of Jean McEwen — I look at his work on my walls every day — but if challenged I'd have to admit to talking nonsense.

GH: Did it take you a while to find your voice? In *General Ludd* the narrative voice is entirely different from that of any of your other work. There's more of a barb in it, more of a sharp tone.

JM: Well, you're making the assumption that that's my tone or my voice. It's the voice of the narrator. The voice of the narrator in *Private Parts* is very different. The voice of the narrator in "The Years in Exile" very different again.

GH: Is voice important to you in your fiction?

JM: I think it's the centre of all fiction.

GH: How much does life experience form your fiction? Do you

draw upon emotional states and use them to form the work, or do you draw upon autobiographical elements?

JM: Standard answer. The impulse is often autobiographical — the details not necessarily so at all.

GH: Do you follow the traditional shape of the story, the so-called dramatic triangle? With a climax and a denouement, strong narrative hook, or do you like the Clark Blaise, Mavis Gallant kind of story that turns around, goes back inside itself? Or do you just follow your intuition and find the shape of the story as you discover it?

JM: A lot of my early stories were very traditional in form — epiphany stories. The only way I wasn't traditional, perhaps, was that I always worked with great intensity, very close-up. And then I wrote some stories which were less traditional in form and the last story I wrote was even modish — or appeared to be.

Most critics seem to have me pegged as a very traditional writer. I'm not sure why. Stories like "The Teeth of My Father" and "The Eastmill Reception Centre" aren't Katherine Mansfield exactly. But I don't follow any school or manner. To use your word, I just *discover* the right shape.

I write each page 20 times over and it's in that rewriting that I eventually find the shape it has to be. I start with a sentence which I might elaborate and expand for half a page. That elaboration throws off an image, say, which I recognize as being what I wanted from the start. So I scrap the half page and start again from that image and then go on to a second sentence. In that second sentence, the same thing might happen again. It's a process of chipping away endless layers of language.

Of course, I know what the story's "about" before I start. That's more or less irrelevant. What the story's really about is the operation of language.

GH: And how language reveals scenes, images . . .

JM: Exactly. I think some people consider my stories rather pedestrian — full of *detailed*, factual *things*. But those people haven't read closely enough — haven't given their whole attention to those things — because it's out of giving yourself totally to the evoked *thing* that meanings and significances arise. Some of my stories, though concrete, are very mysterious. "Keys and Watercress" is a good example.

That seems to me a persuasively *real* story and real because of its wealth of detail. The watch that the old man holds on his palm, you see. Now, the boring people will say, "Ha! A symbol of Time! And if of Time, then of Mortality!" Whereas, of course, it's a watch. And not *any* watch but a particular kind called a Hunter where you press the winding knob and the silver lid springs open to reveal the face. Everything in my stories is always specific, always real. Symbols *have* no life. Words and the way they're marshalled have life.

GH: Do you double check these details?

JM: Research them?

GH: Do you go back and look at a Hunter and say, 'Ha! I've got it right'?

JM: Sometimes. But not often. Most of these details come from passionately remembered things. I've never been in the boy's situation in "Keys and Watercress". It's all invention. But I can see a watch like that one somewhere in my childhood. I can see it now. The scratches on it, the colour of the glass, the way it had yellowed and discoloured with time. I can see the milled edge of the winding knob, the way the brass bloomed through the worn silver-plating. It's a real watch transferred to an imagined story.

The stuffed lion in the old man's house. I had one myself. I'd bought it in a junk shop and it used to be in my bedroom. Many of my stories are a bringing together of passionately remembered physical detail and a re-ordering of the real into a new order which makes a new kind of real.

GH: Where do stories start for you? With scenes, an image, a character, an object, with an emotional gathering in your heart?

JM: They certainly never start with an idea. There's nothing I want to say to anybody. I want to make people *feel*. I want them to live inside the experience of the story and by doing that, by responding to the story's texture and rhetoric, they'll find that meanings *grow out of* the seemingly meaningless.

Stories can start for me with a sound or a scene or a detail which is dream-like or surrealistic in its intensity. This detail, say, might be remembered from the distant past or it might be something I saw yesterday which jumped at me. I can give you an example of an image that's been with me for two or three weeks that's somehow central to a story I intend writing. And it's simply this — of being in a restaurant with a group of friends and looking down and seeing a tiny gleam of light off the fingernail polish of the woman beside me. You must see this scene very carefully. The lighting is fairly dim. The table has a central pool of almost orange-coloured light and this woman is picking up a fork or something or talking across the table and the narrator sees this hint, this spark of light gleaming off the fingernail.

That comes right at the beginning. I don't know *what* the story is but I suspect it's about a man's restlessness, marital and spiritual. The whole story's somehow right there in capsule form in that opening image. That little light is somehow very romantic, very alluring, but illusory. Seems to suggest itself to me as being an *ignis fatuus* which will lead him into spiritual peril.

I get so excited just thinking about it. Lovely. I hope it doesn't go away.

GH: Where do your characters come from? How do you bring your characters to move through the story?

JM: I don't know where characters come from. I'd say they usually come somehow from voices. Whenever I read detective stories or thrillers — those kinds of books which tell you for half a page what someone looks like — I always skip that description because I can never really visualize the person. On the other hand, the character's only got to speak two or three sentences and I get a fairly immediate mental picture of what they look like. Dialogue works so quickly to invent character. And the voice, the vocabulary, the rhythms, the sentence patterns — everything they say *implies* their past history, social status, education, etc. etc. So I work back from the voice to be able to see them clearly. The voices will tell you everything if you'll only listen.

GH: Do you think in sequences of stories, interlocked stories?

JM: I'm pleased you asked that. There seems to be a vogue in Canada for sequences of stories and I think I know exactly why. It's because it turns the story collection into something that's just a touch closer to a novel. I *think* — I wouldn't swear to this — that editors have put pressure on writers to turn collections into pseudo-novels. I have a strong feeling that that happened to Alice Munro and I recall vaguely Margaret Laurence telling me that there'd been some sort of pressure involving *A Bird in the House*.

As far as I'm concerned, the glory of writing stories is that you can write from the point of view of a 5-year old, an 18-year old, male, female, hermaphrodite — all within the covers of one book. An endless display of different forms of rhetoric. Hugh Hood got one off in *None Genuine Without This Signature* — a story called "Gone Three Days" which operates in the "language" of a severely retarded boy. I listened to him perform it when we were reading together at the University of Maine and came close to tears.

Different rhetorics, amazingly different and various worlds, different voices — that's the joy of a story collection. I just can't see why one would wish to restrict oneself to eight stories about the same character or eight stories about alienation in Hamilton, Ont.

It's a disguised demand for a novel, for a "good read" — and a "good read" all too often means fodder to be consumed.

People have said to me personally and in reviews that the weakness of my story collections is that dominant themes — my "philosophy of life" — aren't evident. Well, I haven't *got* a "philosophy of life". If I had, I'd bottle it. But you see what that criticism means, don't you? It means that the reader isn't reading the stories *as stories*.

Surely the only way of judging a collection of stories is by asking if each story, individually, succeeds in creating a real world, if each one, individually, is an entrancing performance. And if it does and if it is, in God's name, what more could you ask for?

GH: So, in fact, that's what connects all your works?

JM: There might well be more. I'm not a critic. But for me, the one demand is that the work be done well. This desire for an expressed "philosophy" seems to me basically philistine. Or French.

I'm reminded of a summer I taught a short story course at the University of Montreal — I was standing in for Hugh Hood. Amazing experience. All the students were French Canadian, of course. Now, I have no time at all for French Canadian stories. They're not stories at all in our sense of the term and I wish people would stop pretending they are. They're completely alien to our understanding of what a story is. They're just silly *contes*. Fantasies, allegories, parables, "think"-stuff. And as far as I'm concerned, about as fascinating as All Bran. I know you're an aficionado and I'm not trying to be irritating but I think it's silly to pretend that English and French minds are even vaguely alike.

Anyway, what happened in this class was most instructive. For me. I don't know about *them*. We were to read stories by Joyce, Greene, and Lawrence. I started with Joyce. And was stuck on one story for three weeks.

"What," they kept on demanding, "is its philosophy?"

"It doesn't *have* a fucking philosophy!"

"But it must!"

"Savour the description of the colour of the old priest's coat."

"What is the coat's *significance*?"

"It's a coat. He wants you to see it. Smell it. That's all. It's a *coat*."

Silence.

"Give us a clue."

But the redeeming feature of the course was D. H. Lawrence. He *did* have a philosophy and they greatly appreciated its repetition three times per page. Lawrence, they concluded, was good. Joyce, bad.

Me — I took the money and ran.

GH: Do you feel more comfortable with short stories than novels?

JM: Yes, definitely. I like the novella form, too. I've said this often before — that the story form is close to poetry. With a novel, you can chuck in bits and pieces of anything that appeals to you. You can expand scenes outrageously if you like them or truncate them if they're boring you and nobody really seems to notice. With a story, you've got to get it dead right. A beat or two off and it's ruined. I just cannot control language and shape over 300 pages the way I can over 20.

GH: How do you feel about your last novel, *General Ludd*?

JM: Mixed feelings. It's most probably a failure as a cohesive work of art. I was insufficiently distanced. Yet, on the other hand, I think it contains chunks which are funnier than anything that's ever been written in Canada. Which isn't a particularly arrogant or immodest comment when you consider the competition. I think the book's probably worth preserving for the nightclub scene, the chapter with Julia Hetherington, the Russian writers — and a few other odds and sods. But Flaubert it ain't.

GH: You often use women characters to bring out the softer aspects of the male characters. And in fact Jim and Kathy's relationship in *General Ludd* is one of your most successful.

JM: Well, that doesn't say much for earlier relationships. It's probably a suicidal thing to do in our literary climate but I want to be honest about the book. I don't need critics to tell me the book's flaws. I've got a more lively awareness about my own work than they have. And I judge my work by comparing it with the best, with the *great* comic writers — Naipaul, Waugh, Waterhouse, etc.

It's a troubled book. I was setting out to write comedy, dark comedy admittedly, but somehow got overmastered by rage so that there's a blurring between Jim Wells as character and me as writer. And this pulls the book out of sharp focus. I wish it were a better book. But the next one will be because I learned a lot from writing *Ludd*.

But you were talking about Kathy. I was unhappy about her all the way through the writing. She isn't realized well. I feel she's very much a lay figure, as it were. The problem for me was that the book was Jim's voice. Kathy was more or less a plot device, a balancing force of reason, a counterweight. But I didn't *care* about her. She wasn't real to me. She wasn't *alive* in the way that Julia Hetherington's alive. I loved that Julia chapter — all those deranged kids — and the way it turns emotional direction at the end becoming quietly sad. *Beautiful* writing.

When I started the book, I started in the third person. This would have given me greater balance and distanced the book. I got about 30 pages in in the third person and then discovered that the book wasn't as zippy as I wanted. It was a bit staid, a bit soggy. But in the first person, I seemed somehow to be tapping into wild energy. It was a trade-off. Zip for balance.

But I don't mind that the book's less than perfect because in doing it I learned a great deal about my weaknesses and strengths. It crystalized for me some important ideas or feelings about character.

GH: Can you expand on that?

JM: Sure. I realized through writing *Ludd* that what really *delights* me is caricature and cartoon. And I'm thinking now of ways of applying caricature to the story form. I think the thing that saves *Ludd*, for me, is the series of portraits — Dr. Bhadwaj, Dick and

Julia Hetherington and their kids, Itzic, Mary Merton, the Colonel, the Russian writers, Cosimo O'Gorman, the pawnbroker, the taxi-driver with the mind like a computer. All these gave me delight. Other parts of the book were willed.

I realized, you see, just *how* deeply interested I've always been in the old tradition. Just as Dickens was. As Waugh was. Commedia figures. Humours. Grotesques. Which is probably why I find V. Woolf unreadable.

The old naming tradition isn't played-out — not by a long way. It's more compelling than all the psychological claptrap. Not that I'd go quite so far as to call someone Squire Allworthy or Sir Epicure Mammon — or dammit, maybe I would. Why not? This has got nothing to do with anything but talking about *names* — I've just thought of that gorgeous name in Alice's "Dance of the Happy Shades", that horrid woman at the party. Alice describes her as smelling "unfresh". What a masterly word! A lesser writer would have been specific there. And this unfresh woman is called Mrs. Clegg. Isn't that lovely? Pinned and wriggling right there.

GH: One last question: Where are you taking your fiction now? Or where is your fiction taking you?

JM: As I was saying a minute ago, I'm brooding about caricature and all the implications of that. It suggests extensive formal changes. I suspect I'm working up to something *broadly* comic. But it will most likely be stories or novellas. Whatever, that's two books ahead.

At the moment, I'm writing a short story. And when I've finished that story, I'm going to write another story which will be entirely unrelated to it. And when I finish that one, another entirely unrelated to that, and so on. Until I've put together enough to make a book which will be greeted by reviewers in the usual manner:

"Technically accomplished, but Metcalf lacks overall vision".

I'm exploring, as I've always been exploring so far as I can see, ways of playing with language, with rhetoric, to make my worlds, in the plural, real and compelling.

Noddy and Big Ears Meet Malvolio

MANY AUTOBIOGRAPHIES OF WRITERS present a picture of a shy and lonely child delivered from solitude and unsympathetic surroundings by the power of the Word, the child's mind captured, for example, by the illustrations in Foxe's *Book of Martyrs* or struggling with the text of the only book in the house, *Pilgrim's Progress*. Good examples of this typical type of experience are recorded in James Laver's *Museum Piece* and in Jocelyn Brooke's *The Military Orchid*.

My own childhood was nothing like this. I cannot remember a time when I was not surrounded by books. My father, a Methodist minister, had a fairly large library, most of the volumes, to be sure, theological, but he also had most of the standard poets and first editions of the novels of Conrad and Hardy. Among the more 'modern' poets, he owned Masefield, Housman, Chesterton, Belloc, Yeats, and Blunden. After he died and I was looking through what books my mother had not promptly donated to Oxfam, I was amazed to find Wilde's *De Profundis*. I'd probably seen it when younger but thought it to be a work of theology.

My mother read all the time. Her reading wasn't 'literary'. Her favourite material was historical novels and detective stories. These came from the Public Library, from Boot's Lending Library, and from Timothy White's Lending Library. The historical novels were of the Georgette Heyer variety, the detective stories by Dorothy L. Sayers, Agatha Christie, Margery Allingham, Ngaio Marsh etc. etc. I associate all these writers, whom I loathe, with the smell of bath-salts and talc, doubtless an early memory of trips to Boots Chemists.

(These detective story writers seem to me, now, to mirror and perpetuate the genuine ghastliness of British middle-class life.)

Reading quickly became an addiction and has remained so. If a day passes without my settling down for three hours with a book, *any* book, I become distressed and irritable. Books, I'm afraid, are a 'fix'. This distress is compounded if I've spent the

29

evening with people or been to the cinema. Then I usually read two books or even three until I'm so exhausted I can fall asleep quickly. The best books for this purpose are thrillers. I read hundreds every year. And incredibly bad stuff they are too.

When I was a child, I also read quickly, the average time for a book being about two hours. On wet days I read my ration of library books in one gulp and often returned in the evening for three more. On the other hand, I was eleven before I could tell time.

Birthdays and Christmas and the visits of relatives were marked by gifts of books. I also acquired books at jumble sales and church bazaars where, because I was my father's son, I was allowed to select what I wanted before the doors were opened. These books were the usual fare — annuals, the 'William' books, Biggles, Worrals, the Arthur Ransome stories, the Rupert annuals which I read, for reasons unknown, until I was in my teens. Tarzan, too. But not one of these books stands out in memory as vastly important simply because I read so much.

Later, gifts of books changed to book-tokens which was much nicer because it meant you could spend hours in bookshops in agonies of decision.

Oddly enough, all this reading did not mean that I was "bookish"; quite the reverse was true. School always baffled me. I'd like to pretend that I was so brilliant I was bored by school. But that isn't true. I was baffled. The only subject in which I did well was English and I only did well in that because I did it automatically. When it came to grammar and parsing, I had no idea of what people were talking about. It took lessons in Latin years later to drive home what was meant by 'noun' and 'adverb'. Math was, and has remained, an entirely closed book.

I passed what was called the "eleven-plus" exam — an instrument for sorting out grammar school hopefuls from "secondary modern" fodder — only because my mother drilled me in "sums" and suchlike.

It quickly became apparent that if I were ever to do anything at all in life it would be on the "arts" side of affairs — though any prospects whatever seemed more than doubtful. At thirteen, I was declared ineducable in Math and I stopped taking the subject altogether. The fact that my Math teacher that year was abnormally small and looked like a Japanese sniper and drove home his points with the rung of a chair may have had *something* to do with it. But not much. The truth is that numbers cause a pain in my forehead.

It's interesting that if I'd been educated in Canada I'd never have reached university because I'd never have passed the requirements in Math. In England it was permissible to replace Math by a Science subject. Physics and Chemistry were as incomprehensible to me as Math. Math, I could see, did somehow relate to life; there were all those problems about how much paper you'd need to paper a room eighty-three feet long with eight dormer windows. But physics! As far as I could see all it involved was lowering weights on bits of string into calibrated tubes of water to see how much overflowed. I couldn't understand why anyone would *wish* to know that. Chemistry was a touch more entertaining because of the fire and smoke but I never seemed able to grasp the *motives* for these activities.

Physics and Chemistry, then, being incomprehensible, left only Biology. I spent most of my free time — alone but not lonely — watching animals, hunting for snakes, searching for fossils, and fishing. I could have taken the Biology teacher to the one locality in Hampshire where smooth snakes were to be found, where bee orchids grew, where the lampreys gathered, where there were the sets, earths, and holts of badgers, foxes, and otters, but all this, I quickly realized, was nothing to do with Biology. Biology was copying diagrams.

School ground on towards my fourteenth year. I did badly in everything except English. Even my toast-rack in woodwork took two years and about three hundred feet of lumber.

The English teaching I received between the ages of twelve and fourteen was, I realize now, superb. Our only activities were précis, paraphrase, exercises in comprehension, and essay writing. In other words, we were drilled in logic, in the steel structure of the language. Literature was dealt with in the following way: each term we were given a list of twelve novels to read at home. This meant that in a school year we read a minimum of thirty-six novels. At the end of each term we were given a test cunningly designed to reveal if we had in fact read them.

'With whom did Jim Davis shelter after the fight with the revenue officers?'

The following books were on those lists and suggest the

general flavour of the reading: *Jim Davis, Treasure Island, Kidnapped, King Solomon's Mines, The History of Mr. Polly, A Tale of Two Cities, Tarkar the Otter, Oliver Twist, Allan Quartermain, Kim, David Copperfield, Three Men in a Boat, Prester John, The Thirty-Nine Steps, Rodney Stone, The White Company, The Cloister and the Hearth, Rookwood, Old St. Paul's* etc. etc.

All good stuff and entertaining. The idea of discussing such things as plot and characterization would never have occurred to my teachers.

And a damn good thing too.

(I suspect that, nowadays, these books would be considered far too difficult in syntax and vocabulary and entirely lacking in *relevance*. I prefer them however, to the books tailored to adolescent interests with titles like *Jennifer's First Period*.)

This, then, was my "official" life until I was fourteen.

But I have another set of memories covering the same years which I realize now, groping back, are the *really* important ones.

They are disjointed.

Very early, being with my father in Foyle's. He is searching along the bottom rows of second-hand tomes in theology. We are in a basement, in a canyon of books. We are both glazed black with that peculiar kind of muck that grows on old books. My father has bought me a book to keep me quiet as he roots and rummages. It is *Struwwelpeter* with the horrifying illustration of the leaping man cutting off the child's thumb. Afterwards, we have tea in a Lyon's Corner House.

(Many years later, floundering in the minatory obscurities of early Auden, I read with shocked understanding:

The bolt is sliding in its groove;
    Outside the window is the black remover's van:
    And now with sudden swift emergence
    Come the hooded women, the hump-backed surgeons,
And the Scissor Man.)

Another memory of my father, a man I wish I'd known. He was a distant figure, not given to conversation, eccentric. Being a

Methodist minister, he was relatively impoverished. Money was never thrown around. It was, in fact, pinched. On a rare summer holiday in Swanage we were walking past a junk shop. In the window hung a blown-up, varnished Blow-Fish, a prickly globe of wonder. In we went. The fish was two shillings and sixpence. My father bought it for me. He also bought me some bound volumes of an illustrated magazine which formed a history of the First World War. And, as we were about to leave, he pointed out the sword of a sword-fish and suggested that it was, if not rare, then at least unusual, and precisely the sort of thing that if passed up would remain a source of regret for ever after.

This was not condescension on his part nor, I suspect, a desire to please a small boy. He was never "nice" in that way. It was a seriously held opinion.

Later, a collection of *Superman* and *Combat* comics, real American ones with shiny covers, not the dowdy British reproductions. These desirables were the stakes in games of marbles and nearest-to-the-wall with cigarette cards.

Later still, *Boy's Own Paper*, all kept in severe order by volume and number.

Collecting, then. My father collected obscure books on theological matters. My brother collected coins — a harmless hobby which led eventually to his present activities at the Ashmolean Museum and a world reputation as a scholar in numismatics and monetary history.

When I was small, my brother had a museum full of coins, fossils, mineral specimens, pottery shards, and curious objects such as hair from an elephant's tail. At first the museum was in his bedroom but it later expanded into a disused pantry; you had to pay ½d to see it. He also put out a weekly newspaper produced on a jelly pad; this also cost ½d.

All sorts of 'antiques' and curios were cheaper then and far more readily available than now. I had small collections of swords and pistols. At about the age of ten I had acquired, by swapping, a 'horse pistol' — a battered percussion cap job — and a bullet mould. I began an obsessive manufacture of lead bullets in the kitchen using one of my mother's saucepans. I have scars on my hands to this day from molten lead. I cycled all the way from Bournemouth to Ringwood to buy a tin of percussion caps from a gunsmith. But the powder defeated me; I couldn't get the mixture right.

My passion for bullet-making led me into crime. I was apprehended removing lengths of lead plumbing that were still attached to houses.

My brother grew copper sulphate crystals in pie dishes and mineral gardens under water-glass in Mason jars.

My father steeped his home-grown tobacco in other domestic utensils and 'cooked' it in the oven.

My mother bewailed the state of her pots and pans and, I suspect, suffered something close to a breakdown as the house filled with coins, books, snakes, nature specimens, hedgehogs, ammonites, belemnites, trilobites, caterpillars, butterflies, moths, setting-boards, nets, killing-jars, stone age hand-axes, sand lizards and slow-worms, *The Observer Book* of Trees, Wild Flowers, Birds, Reptiles . . . volume after volume in *The British Naturalist* series, owl pellets, fishing tackle, seething trays of gentles, hypodermic syringes and formaldehyde and cloudy jars sealed with sealing-wax containing newts, leeches, lizards, ticks, and various internal organs.

Setting-boards, the rust-proof black pins, the cork-lined exhibition cases — all came by mail from an emporium in South London. The catalogue of this store featured treasures beyond the dreams of avarice — fossils, arrowheads, scrapers, axes (the *polished* ones), Roman terracotta lamps, sundry wondrous antiquities. The very *name* of this store, which I've never visited, had the same effect on me as Chimborazo and Cotopaxi had on the boy in Walter J. Turner's poem "Romance"; it was called Watkins and Doncaster.

(On my first return from Canada to visit my mother she confided one afternoon that she was very worried about some shotgun shells that the tide of collecting had deposited in a cupboard some twelve years earlier. She was worried that they would explode. She said they often made her feel low and that she wept thinking about them. Amazed, I asked her why she hadn't thrown them out. She said that she hadn't wanted "the blood of the dustbin men on her conscience". And if that isn't a detail from a Thurber story, I don't know what is.)

I'm talking about collecting at such length because I think it's intimately connected with writing. With mine, certainly. There is an affinity between the two activities. The *kind* of knowledge that comes out of collecting differs from purely formal knowledge. It is knowledge informed by love and lust. And a part of that love comes from *ownership*. Collecting then, the attendant reading and the resultant judgement — it's all an intricate *aesthetic* affair. A love of books is not simply a love of writing, of stories. It's a love of paper, binding, and print. A real love of books can't be fostered by *libraries*; they're useful, of course, but the relationship can never be a love relationship. Libraries are rather like 'houses of convenience'.

So far as I can remember, there were no paperbacks when I was small. To this day I dislike them. They are not really *books*. I buy and read many of them, of course, but if I run across a book that moves me deeply I make it my immediate business to acquire a hardcover and, preferably, a first edition. Thus recently, I've spent ages with catalogues and international correspondence acquiring first editions of Paul Scott's *Staying On*, Naipaul's *In a Free State*, and Beryl Bainbridge's *Injury Time*. There is a large element here of *honouring* the work of the writer. For similar reasons, I recently bought for 99 cents each many remaindered copies of a novel by Richard Yates. It distressed me profoundly to find Richard Yates *in Woolco*.

(An educational aside — before I came to Canada I'd never heard the expression 'time to crack the books'. It says a great deal.)

Collecting has other important links with writing. It forces the use of the eyes. It is tactile. It conserves. It is comparative. It inevitably turns the collector back into the past thus forging intimate bonds with history and enlarging through love the historical sense. It enforces contact with the real.

The collector is usually seen by the non-collector as obsessive and harmlessly loony but I hold that whether he collects Regency furniture or hand-painted chamber-pots, the collector's real is more real than yours. Simply, he *sees* more.

The next two phases of my adolescent reading fall into periods marked out by my school career and the external "Ordinary" and "Advanced Level" examinations.

The "Ordinary Level" exams are, or were, equivalent to Canadian high school matriculation and are usually sat at age sixteen. For some they are the end of secondary school, for others another winnowing process to be followed by "Advanced Level" exams and university.

At sixteen I was still mutedly unhappy and unsuccessful at school. I was used to being told I was dim and thick and had come to believe it. My brother, Cambridge now years behind him, had been and continued to be unbelievably brilliant. My school career was compared at all points with his and was found wanting. At sixteen I was under the spell of Charles Atlas and had decided that I wanted to be a professional boxer.

(Early influence of *Rodney Stone* and Pierce Egan?)

The smell of sweat, leather, and rosin captivated me. I faithfully performed Charles Atlas' secret exercises. Under the guidance of an ex-sergeant — 'Partial to 'im, are you? Don't '*ug* 'im. '*it* 'im!' — I learned to "work downstairs" as Henry Cooper puts it.

My body was flooded by naughty hormones and the air was heavy with rebellion.

My mother's anguish and pressure increased as the exams drew nearer. The forecasts for my future were grim — on good days I might, if lucky, aspire to become a plumber's mate, on bad days the gallows beckoned. And so, perhaps to please my parents, perhaps simply infected by the prevailing hysteria, I started to work. Everyone was impolitely amazed when I actually passed the damn exams and the letter arrived from the Ministry of Education. My mother, typically, wondered aloud if they'd got my name confused with another Metcalf.

Concurrent with boxing and Ordinary Level exams my interest in books became more passionate. During this year I'd found in Beckenham an auctioneer who held weekly sales. The books which accumulate in any branch of the second-hand trade were displayed in trays outside the sale rooms and offered for 6d per volume. It became my habit to graze there every Saturday and my general rage for books led me to straighten the rows and tidy up after ill-mannered browsers. Sometimes I was taken to be in the employ of the auctioneers and was given sixpences which I always turned over to the man in charge. Eventually we came to an arrangement whereby I kept an eye on the books and collected the money thus liberating him to drink tea and he allowed me four or five books a week in payment.

I built up a collection of Henty in first editions, not because I wanted to read them, but because the appalling colour plates enchanted me. I also acquired a complete collection of W. W. Jacobs, a short story writer who continues to appeal. I came to be able to tell the decade of a book by a glance at its binding.

I still have some of the books I picked up there — a signed volume of poetry called *The Curlew's Cry* by Redwood Anderson — a poet I very recently discovered actually *lived* in Beckenham. I wish I'd known that then because I'd have gone to see him. What an odd meeting *that* would have been! I also found a book called *Tricks of the Trade* by J. C. Squire, a collection of parodies. This delighted me and taught me more about poetry than anyone since. I can say, quite sincerely, that any understanding of poetry I have was sparked by Squire; years of pleasure for 6d.

(Squire is now a largely forgotten figure. He hadn't a clue about modern poetry and resented it when he didn't find it merely comic. His attitude is quite understandable. Thomas Hardy didn't understand Katherine Mansfield's stories and advised her to write more stories about the girls in "The Daughters of the Late Colonel". His own stories are tedious. His sensibility was of his time. Does that diminish his achievement? I *still* feel loyal to Squire.)

These book-tending Saturdays passed in glazed happiness.

The third strand of influence at this time was my brother. He had left behind him in the house James Joyce, T. S. Eliot, D. H. Lawrence etc. I perceived, correctly, that these people stood in opposition to the religious world of my parents and their Georgian poets and 'middlebrow' novelists such as Priestley. As I, too, was by now in opposition to my parents and the middle-class world generally, I started to read the 'moderns' because they seemed to oppose what I opposed and were *not respectable*.

(All this is *historically* interesting. It seems utterly amazing now that as late as the early fifties the 'modernists' could still *épater les bourgeois*, that a reproduction of Van Gogh's yellow chair could still make my mother, and many others like her, decidedly uncomfortable. Eliot was described by an early reviewer as 'a drunken helot' and I suppose he *did* seem what he wasn't if what you were used to was John Masefield. Historically, my taste was formed against a background which still perceived 'the modern' as a threat. What a brief time it has taken for all that glory to fade, for Eliot's star to wane: from what I can gather, he is now widely thought of as a sort of literary Eisenhower.)

And so literature came to mean not only delight in the stuff itself but self-definition through identification. I *had* to see myself in fantasy as a writer or a painter or a gym-fighter because I couldn't bear being what I was. Had my parents been interested in jazz and D. H. Lawrence, I'd probably have become a Methodist minister.

And how I read and postured and pined! Pined for strong drink, *amours*, strange sensation. I discovered Wilde and *A Rebours*. And felt myself more refined, more sensitive, more . . . than the mundane world of my dreary parents with their narrow rectitude.

(How comical to think of a boy vicariously savouring Huysman's caviar while really yearning to get to grips with life's bangers, as it were, and mash.)

My young self causes me endless amusement.

I read Jessie L. Weston's *From Ritual to Romance* and *The Golden Bough* because of the footnotes in *The Waste Land* and then went on to discover ripe old loonies like Dr. Margaret Murray whose *The Witch-Cult in Western Europe* and *The Divine King in England* were much in vogue. These, and such books as *The White Goddess*, doubtless appealed because they were, childishly, anti-Christian. The idea of a harvest festival or spring rite where you gorged until sick and copulated in furrows, repeatedly, struck me as a definite advance on singing "We Plough the Fields and Scatter" in a church full of marrows.

And then I discovered the idea of bibliographies and of following reference and my reading began that meandering course it's followed ever since.

From D. H. Lawrence to Katherine Mansfield to Middleton Murry, to Frieda's ex-husband Ernest Weekley, to Gurdjeff, Ouspensky, Mme Blavatsky, and Annie Besant's *Wisdom of the Upanishads*, to Roger Fry and Clive Bell and Vincent's letters to Theo. From the gibberish of 'Significant Form' forward to the gibberish of Herbert Read and back to Ruskin and Pater and then forward once again to Whistler's *Gentle Art* — on and on unendingly and, in large part, uncomprehendingly.

My life at sixteen was, then, a bizarre confusion, an unlikely grafting of Oscar Wilde and Tom Cribb. At the same time that I was building the Body Beautiful and snuffling blood and mucus in the ring, I was also beginning to burn with a hard, gemlike flame.

I had a splendid hardbound book with marbled end papers, an old business ledger, comically enough, into which I copied — and learned by heart — poems which spoke to my heated condition. I can't remember everything in it now but I do remember chunks of Shakespeare — the description of Ophelia's death, the Florizel and Perdita stuff — bombast from *Tamburlaine* and *Faustus*, "The Lotus-Eaters" — purple passages all and the purpler the better. I liked my poetry all stops out. I had a peculiar passion for De La Mare and still consider him a remarkable poet. Hopkins, of course. Keats, inevitably. Some D. H. Lawrence — some of it *very* good — if only he'd stuck to poems and travel books! And H. D. *Lots* of H. D. and F. S. Flint. Many of Pound's Chinese variations. Arthur Waley, too. A few odd chunks from the Cantos which I then found impressive but now find incomprehensible. And, of course, Dylan Thomas.

I can remember that I started with *Under Milk Wood*. The pure *shock* of reading Thomas for the first time, of reading something like "though moles see fine tonight in the snouting velvet dingles", cannot now be conveyed. I went on to the poems spending hours even on the 'Altarwise by owl-light' sequence. And that is *genuine* dedication.

(Dylan Thomas remained a pernicious influence because when I started to write years later I found myself still seduced by his grammatical transpositions and general flamboyant tinsel. The attack on reputations, though inevitable, always leaves a bad taste in my mouth. Thomas' faults are obvious but he wrote eight or ten poems which will always stay with us and surely to God that's enough? The prose, though it came so easily to him he felt guilty, remains a major accomplishment. *Portrait of the Artist as a Young Dog* is, in my opinion, as good as Joyce. No. To be honest, I enjoy it more. Much as I admire the chasteness of his writing, some of Joyce's stories seem to me now *attenuated*.)

Of all the poetry I read then, the work of the Imagists probably had the greatest impact and the greatest subsequent influence.

The third phase of my adolescent reading followed, vaguely, the work I was supposed to be doing for my "Advanced Level" exams. I was seventeen and eighteen during those two years and studying only two subjects at school — English and History. I had only two classes a day and the rest of the time I was free to read and write essays. I was not even required to *go* to school. The classes were less classes than very friendly seminars. For the first time in my life I was happy at school. What I was *supposed* to do coincided with what I *wanted* to do.

But before going on, I think I need to explain how it came about that I abandoned my desire to become a gym fighter . . .

(Pity, really. I'd have been the first welterweight to burn with a hard and gemlike flame.)

As can be realized from all the confusion of the foregoing, my desire to become a practitioner of the Noble Art or to become Gully Jimson or James Joyce was less a desire to *become* than a desire not to be what I was. I didn't really know *what* I wanted. I was, secretly, open to offers.

After the results of the "Ordinary Level" exams were known, I was summoned by the Headmaster. His name was Mr. White. I have no idea of his Christian name; everyone was so in awe of him that I suppose we thought he hadn't got one. I had achieved some sort of distinction in English on those exams and Mr. White flatly *informed* me that I was going to go to university to study English. My previous general dimness had precluded any study of Latin. To get into a university to study English, Latin was a prerequisite. Mr. White said that despite my earlier criminality and stubborn stupidity — he alluded to certain incidents — he sensed in me abilities as yet untapped. It was his intention to coach me in Latin every day from scratch to the set books in one year.

It was the first time that *I* believed that someone believed in me.

Simply because of this, I threw myself into the work with great determination and growing pleasure. I learned enough Latin to develop a keen regret that I hadn't been taught Greek and Latin from my tender years. I learned more English, and more about literature, during that year of Latin than in all the years preceding.

(I regret also my inability to speak French. I've always felt the non-speaking of English to be comically unnatural but recognize this as prejudice. I was *taught* French, of course, but by a Welshman from Cardiff who infused the language with a singular sing-song which makes anything I say absolutely incomprehensible except to a French-speaking Welshman.)

There were only seven students in the English class, all of them very bright, and we were fortunate in our English teacher, a double-first from Cambridge, a serious man with a great love of literature. The set books were works by Chaucer and Shakespeare and a representative clutch of writers from the Romantic period — Wordsworth, Blake, Keats, Byron, and Jane Austen — but these were merely a framework. I read more in those two years than I'd ever read before. It's impossible to convey the intellectual excitement of those two years; we were in a sort of intellectual and emotional pressure-cooker.

Our teacher concentrated on close reading of the texts. The placing of the texts in a larger framework was left entirely to us. The reading we did was entirely unsupervised; it was simply assumed that we would read widely and with passion. I read all day and far into the nights; the weekly essays on subjects of our own choosing provided an opportunity to marshal and organize new information and ideas.

I'll try to suggest the breathless, careering insanity of the reading. Starting *Northanger Abbey*, the teacher suggested the obvious point that one couldn't really approach it without knowing what was being parodied — which led to *The Castle of Otranto*, *The Monk*, Lewis' *Tales of Terror*, *Vathek*, *Rasselas*, *The Mysteries of Udolpho*, *The Italian*, *Melmoth the Wanderer*, dire tomes such as Praz's *The Romantic Agony*. Which led to Byron. To Quennell. To revolutions. To Garibaldi, Bolivar, Marx, Proudhon, Bakunin, and Kropotkin. Background books like Watt's *The Rise of the Novel* which led, in turn, back to previously unread novels — lesser Defoe, *filthy* Samuel Richardson, the minor Fielding, Smollett, the *other* Sterne. And somehow forward to the diaries of the Austen period — marvellous gobs of gossip — to Captain Jesse's *Life of Brummel*, the mystic doings of Lady Hester Stanhope, to T. H. White's *The Age of Scandal* and then, of course, like a homing pigeon to White himself who led back to Malory who led to the *Mabinogion* which somehow led to Robert Graves who in turn led back to Greece and Rome and archeology — Mortimer Wheeler, Sir Arthur Evans, Michael Ventris, obscure papers on Cycladic figures, the Rosetta Stone, Napoleon again, fast detour through the Revolution with side trips to de Sade and a glance at *Venus in Furs*, back to Arthur Bryant's popular history of the Peninsular Campaign, on and on and on.

The same sort of thing with Blake. Off to Swedenborg. To engraving. Back to Hogarth. Forward to Samuel Palmer and Stanley Spencer. Back to British Israelites, to Sir Joshua Reynolds' *Discourses*, to the 1831 *Life* of Henry Fuseli, to Gilchrist's *Life* of Blake himself. Side trips to John Wilkes — what *was* the connection? — to Fox and Pitt. Stubbornly back to the texts themselves. Baffled.

What a relief it was when an eminent professor at university said in a seminar group,

"What would you say was the *key* to William Blake?"

'My God!' I thought. 'Is there a key? Something vital I *haven't* read?'

Into the literary silence, he said,

"Well, the key thing about Blake was that he was potty."

I've often thought about those two years and wondered where the energy came from. I can only suppose it was repressed sexuality. I suppose this experience of reading is exactly the same as most other people's but I cannot forget the *intensity* of it all, the daily expansion of knowledge.

Just before I went to university, my father was transferred from Beckenham to Leicester, an unlovely city. Walking home one day from the city museum which had some paintings and drawings by Ardizzione which attracted me, I passed what seemed to be a private house but which had a small sign in the window advertising books. I opened the front door and found myself in an entrance hall literally *piled* with antiquarian books — acres of old leather stretched before me. Just off this hall was what had been a sitting room. It was now a cave of books and sitting at a desk was a very Dickensian character in rumpled cardigan, *muffler*, and tobacco ash. He peered over his spectacles and nodded.

For mere shillings, I bought a copy of Stow's *Chronicles* (1589) and contemporary editions in calf of *Tom Jones*, Mackenzie's *The*

Man of Feeling, Graves' *The Spiritual Quixote*, *Roderick Random*, and a disbound first edition of *The Corsair*.

The man, middle-aged but looking old, was the surviving Halliday brother, as I soon discovered one of the most well-known and scholarly of antiquarian dealers. His catalogues were a feast. We soon became quite friendly and I was given the run of his stock. I would take volumes to him, excavated from the filthy piles, picked up off the floor, and he would say,

"So *that's* where that went. Well! Well! Interesting old book that. Russian. St. John Chrysostom. Parchment and written in a nice hand. How much? Oh, I don't know . . . I could let you have it for twenty-five thousand . . . ."

He gave me what in the trade are called "reading" or "working" copies (i.e., damaged) of anonymous eighteenth-century novels — many of them "By a lady".

Anonymous novels are catalogued (incompletely) in a work by Halkett and Laing entitled *A Dictionary of the Anonymous and Pseudonymous Literature of Great Britain*. I've never read any kind of survey which talks about them *as literature*. During those visits in that filthy house with the musty smell of old leather and old paper in my nostrils, I saw a project before me of reading those novels in Halkett and Laing and writing on them as literature, as the matrix, as it were, from which rose the peaks of Richardson, Fielding, Smollett, Sterne . . .

This house and Mr. Halliday himself focussed all the strains in my character which respond to the past more strongly than to the present or future and my reading now included the catalogues of Quaritch, Maggs, Rota, etc. etc. I wallowed in bindings and leathers and fonts, in all the lovely jargon of the trade, half-titles, colophons, foxing, black letter, washed leaves . . .

University turned out to be something of an anti-climax. I found when I got there that I'd done it all. Certainly there was plenty I hadn't read so I read it but it was all rather a let-down after the intimacy and passion of that sixth-form class. I dutifully learned Anglo-Saxon and read the unfascinating voyages of those sons of fun Ohthere and Wulfstan. I plugged gaps. But my heart wasn't in it. I was far too busy drinking, fornicating,

43

rock-climbing, indulging my taste for antiquarian books, being, in general, prodigal. I was also busy *cultivating* tastes — wine, bullfights in Pamplona, the paintings of William Scott who taught in nearby Bath, theatre, food, and the company of small-time criminals, mostly Jamaican, who lived by breaking and entering and, in one case, by starring in extremely rude movies — but these are unchaste memories.

I was not actually *gripped* by Anglo-Saxon, Middle English, vowel-shifts, and other such linguistic *crotte*. Formal literature teaching ended pretty much at Tennyson. There was, I seem to remember, a seminar of Leavisite persuasion that twittered on about Lawrence but by then it had penetrated even my dim mind that Lawrence was not only boring but *wrote badly*.

(I used to review books for the university newspaper and reviewed *Lady Chat* when it appeared in all its unexpurgated tedium. Because I *quoted* from the dreary book, the editor of the paper was disciplined by the university's Registrar and my expulsion from the university mooted. The Registrar was a peppery ex-Army officer and I was intemperate enough to suggest that a man of his background ought to be inured to sodomy.)

I sought relief from Professor L. C. Knight and his dessicated crew in reading novels, an activity that came close to being considered frivolous.

I first read Joyce Cary's *The Horse's Mouth* while at university and was stunned. I was even more overwhelmed when I read the other two books in the trilogy. I have never understood why Cary's reputation has remained so low among the critical fraternity unless it is that the books run, essentially, against the 'modernist' current. All of Cary's books (perhaps with the exception of his collection of short stories) are interesting; some are superb. My favourites were the books in the two trilogies, *Mr. Johnson*, and *Charley Is My Darling*. I was much influenced by his theories of characterization finding them much more persuasive than the prevailing 'psychological' orthodoxies.

(The introductions that Cary wrote to the *Carfax* editions of the novels are extremely interesting as are his Clark Lectures which were published under the title *Art & Reality*.)

America did not really impinge much on the British literary mind except, of course, for Hemingway, Faulkner, and Fitzgerald. I had read Hemingway long before university but returned again and again to the short stories. Hemingway has been an indescribable world influence so there's no need to go into *that* — except to protest the way that his foibles and insanities are pressed into service to invalidate his art. I actually met him in, of all places, Pamplona. He was following Dominguin and writing "The Dangerous Summer". I was callow enough to go up to him in the street and tell him I really, *really* liked his stuff. He had a beer. He was amazingly tolerant.

(I find nowadays that an alarming number of students haven't read Hemingway. This is particularly true of females. They say, 'Well, he's so macho, isn't he?')

When I was a student, the short story was not a form that was studied in school or university. Perhaps things have changed. The only story writer who was 'officially' recognized was Katherine Mansfield. The story was considered a foreign form — Russian, French, American. I had to wait until coming to Canada to discover Ring Lardner and Eudora Welty and the story writers of the American South.

(Even in Canadian universities there seems to be a prejudice against stories. It's true that they're taught everywhere but graduate committees, so I'm told, shy away from theses on story writers — not enough *body* to stories apparently, unless they're by the suitably dead and inept.)

Nathanael West was *first* published in England while I was a student, the four books bound together in one fat feast. (And, what's more, he was not published by a major publisher.) The horror of the history of West's publishing fortunes is not unlike the progressive dismemberment of L. Pitkin.

Another writer who meant a great deal to me, and still does, is Keith Waterhouse. I have read *Jubb* countless times and consider it a book of the utmost moral and artistic importance. I came across the book, I recall, in a Publishers' Remainder Sale held to celebrate National Book Week.

But more important to me than any other was, and is, Evelyn Waugh, a writer who *delights* and about whose stylistic brilliance there is nothing I wish to say.

(In recent years, as the Sykes biography has appeared and the Letters and Diaries, I have come to love the man too. Those reviewers who dismissed the Diaries as the portrait of a gross, selfish, self-pitying drunk missed a large part of the fun for Waugh's life was as much an invention as his fiction. The complexity of evaluating Waugh's invented life as recorded by Waugh should have given those hasty reviewers pause. Waugh obviously derived great pleasure from watching himself playing the role of Himself. There were in him many suggestions of Basil Seal. He was rather like Toad of Toad's Hall — "always mastered by his imagination".)

These writers, then, stand out sharply from the hundreds I doubtless read during those years. I can see similarities beneath the very obvious differences. All influenced me profoundly.

At the end of my time at university I was reluctant to leave. There was no future that I could imagine. Friends and acquaintances were moving into research, the BBC, the wine trade, oil companies, and advertising. One turncoat even entered upon a career with Barclay's Bank. Not one of these prospects could have tempted me to roll out of bed. To prolong sunlit days and a pleasant life in a slum, but a *Georgian* slum, I drifted into the buffooneries of a Certificate in Education. From there I drifted with rather forced enthusiasm into teaching where for a couple of years I attempted to plumb the secondary-modern mind. I drifted to Canada.

It was quite a long time before I *dared* to think of writing.

The Yellow School Bus

ON OCTOBER 31ST 1980 at the Park Plaza Hotel in Toronto I was the Banquet Speaker at the Annual Fall Conference of the Ontario Council of Teachers of English. The main dish was Roast Stuffed Cornish Game Hen with Woodland Herb Dressing, Baby Carrots, and Wild Rice.

The following address, delivered on Halloween, was received more as trick than treat.

My host, the President of the Ontario Council of Teachers of English, in an astounding display, rushed to the lectern the moment I'd finished and burst into an incoherent tirade assuring the audience that I was fundamentally mistaken in everything I'd said and that I couldn't have meant any of it anyway and that he'd like to hit me with a bottle.

Later in the festivities, I was asked by John Stevenson, editor of *Indirections*, the magazine of the Ontario Council of Teachers of English, if I would send him my speech for publication. Two days later I wrote to him at the address he had given me to explore, politely, the possibilities of remuneration.

I did not receive a reply.

Writers are haunted by a myth from an earlier world, a myth which still whispers to them and leaves them always disappointed. The shape of the myth remains astonishingly clear. Here is its outline.

A talented young writer submits a short story to a prestigious literary magazine. The story is accepted. It is discussed and praised by a discriminating audience. The young writer is invited to lunch at a fashionable restaurant by the famous and eccentric editor of the magazine who over endless courses regales the young writer with loud and scabrous tales of the doings of his elders and betters in the literary world and does endearingly eccentric things such as tucking the tablecloth into the neck of his shirt. During lunch, and by arrangement, a famous publisher joins them. He is addressed by the magazine's editor as Spotty or Buff-Buff or some similar unlikely endearment.

They were at school together.

Cognac is swilled. The afternoon somehow ends at the publisher's office with the young writer clutching a contract for a collection of stories, or more amazingly, a collection of travel pieces or *feuilletons*.

This beginning is recalled in endless memoirs.

The myth continues.

Buff-Buff has in his employ another eccentric editor of near genius who fosters this budding talent, castigates, coaxes. The relationship between the young writer and the editor quickly becomes that of son to beloved father. The first book appears and is charitably reviewed in important places. The book does not, however, sell. The publisher, entirely undismayed, urges the young writer to retire to a country cottage, there to concentrate all his powers on a second work.

(The sum necessary to maintain young writer and wife without undue privation and with drinkable wine and a spot of rough shooting thrown in rises during the twenties and thirties from £30 to £150 per annum. This sum is cheerfully supplied by the publisher in the form of an advance or slightly less cheerfully in the form of an allowance by the writer's father.)

Slowly, the books appear. None sells in vast numbers but sales are respectable. The writer is building a solid reputation as an important literary figure. He has a following. The stories and novels are kept in print, are reprinted in small numbers. His work is reissued in cheap editions. The publisher, who had invested in the idea of a career rather than in a single book, is repaid; his firm glows with the lustre of Literary Worth. These respectable books, these worthy books, books essential in a civilized community, are eventually given the final accolade of publication in a Uniform Edition.

Literature has been served and the books were in any case subsidized by the rather distressing but profitable romances written by ghastly ladies who live in Cotswold manor houses.

And then to bring the myth full circle — one day the writer reads in a literary magazine a striking story. The name rings a bell. He hunts through back issues and finds other stories he'd overlooked before. The language is promising, a few images haunting. He phones the editor and his publisher. They invite the young author to a bibulous lunch where in a borrowed suit he dines on the indiscreet gossip of his elders and betters . . .

The main outlines of the myth are here: the idea of a tradition, the belief that talent must be served, the gentlemanly distaste for trade, the support of a discriminating audience . . .

(I have concentrated on the British form of the myth because until recently Canadian publishing patterned itself after British models. The American version of the myth, more flamboyant and excessive, is not, in essentials, much different except for the writer's early 'romantic' burn-out. The boozy lunches in Soho are there replaced by binges at the offices of Horace Liverwright where three days later drunken bodies are still being found in pianos.)

When I first came to Canada and started writing, the myth still had a kind of half-life. I pestered the editors of literary magazines with my offerings until one day *Prism International*, then being guided by Earle Birney, accepted eight stories all at once.

I had submitted sixteen.

I had lots.

But I was not invited from Montreal to Vancouver for lunch.

Two of these stories were later reprinted in an anthology published by the *Ryerson Press* and this event put me in touch with the Editor of Genius — Earle Toppings. He was not responsible for the anthology. I received the very strong impression that he thought my stories had been selected for inclusion because the editors were Italian with an imperfect grasp of English. I thought then and still think that he is the best editor in Canada. The departure from the myth in this case was, thank God, that Earle Toppings refused to publish or even contemplate publishing any of my work. He knew it was immature and told me so but in a kindly way and with infinite patience and forebearance.

My debt to him is great.

I never did drink away the afternoon with a representative of the *Ryerson Press* nor with Bill Clarke of *Clarke, Irwin* when my first contract was signed. Everything happened by mail. Those boozy lunches in a celebrated restaurant listening to gossip about one's elders and betters are, in the Canadian version of the myth, having coffee with Robert Weaver of the CBC in the coffee shop of the Four Seasons Hotel on Jarvis Street.

And as for all the rest of it — the small but steady sales, the support of a discriminating audience, a career crowned, as it were, by a Uniform Edition . . .

Let us turn from the seduction of the myth and look at reality.

The myth faded in Canada with the collapse of the *Ryerson Press*. *Ryerson* had been the very model of the myth — idealistic, antiquated, charming, gentlemanly, ramshackle and eccentric in a teetotal sort of way. The sale of *Ryerson* in the early seventies to *McGraw-Hill*, located on the ominously named Progress Avenue, provoked a nationalist uproar and during the rest of the decade it seemed that Canadian publishing was getting healthier and healthier. But all this fervent activity was precisely that — the fevered gaiety and strength of the dying consumptive. What had seemed a rebirth was, in fact, an extended death. What everyone had preferred to overlook or steadfastly refused to believe was that in Canada *there was no audience*.

Statistics Canada recently proclaimed that in Canada there are five million functional illiterates. I don't really know how functional illiteracy is defined but in the southern States *literacy* was being equated recently with the ability to recognize a Stop Sign, write your name, and read the label on a can of dog food. The ability to pass this rigorous test does not, of course, guarantee the desire or ability to read *War and Peace*.

For centuries "the Book" has meant the Bible; in my part of the country any mention of "the Book" would be taken as meaning the Sears Catalogue.

The following statistics do not carry the imprimatur of Statistics Canada but they are, essentially, accurate.

The Canadian literary magazine with the largest circulation sells between 1000 and 1300 copies per issue.

A first novel from a major publisher — a novel with good reviews — sells, on average, 1000–1200 copies.

A commercial book such as a thriller does well to sell 4000 copies.

A sale of 1000 copies of a collection of stories is eminently respectable.

A year's hard work will provide a writer not untypically with something in the region of $800.00 in royalties.

(There are few exceptions to these figures. Every year there are, of course, a few books of serious fiction which sell in considerably larger numbers but cynical booksellers have voiced the suspicion that these books, like the ritual grapes, are taken to hospitals.

There are also serious literary artists whose books sell in astonishing numbers for extra-literary reasons. Margaret Atwood and Alice Munro have a large feminist following, a constituency which probably doesn't throw its weight behind, say, Mordecai Richler.)

The talk in the literary world of Canada is now not of "books" but of "product", "units", and "the bottom line". *Macmillan* has stopped publishing poetry. *McClelland and Stewart* with a proud past is racing into a softbound future.

Chain bookstores, the attrition of the independent booksellers, the promotion of the "commercially viable", the vulgar quest for the ultimate Canadian "blockbuster" which will command the highest racks in the nation's grocery stores for three whole weeks . . .

The future seems less than rosy.

It was with bitter amusement that I read in your Programme Highlights of *five* seminars or workshops on Creative Writing. If you and all your members actually *bought* books, it would mean that the total Canadian sale of Canadian books would nearly *double*. And if the members of similar associations in the other provinces actually *bought* books — but this is to be, I realize, visionary.

To be completely sordid, the fee I am being paid for speaking this evening amounts to nearly half the sum I earn annually in royalties. I am not motivated in making these remarks by a personal bunch of sour grapes. Figures not wildly different apply in Canada to such writers as V. S. Naipaul and Mavis Gallant, writers of towering stature.

I noticed that one of your Programme Highlights was entitled *Let's Boogie into Poetry*: it would seem to me far more germane to

51

boogie into the nearest bookshop. My concern is not simply cold cash though writers cannot write without it. My concern is equally with readers, with being read, for without readers there will be no books.

In Canada, we are frighteningly close to that edge.

Poetry, *real* poetry, has been pretty much driven to the wall; it circulates in Canada rather like *samizdat* in Russia. There's a flood of excruciatingly *bad* poetry, of course, therapy stuff, thin gruel by intense young women, in the main, emanating from small presses like Fred Cogswell's *Fiddlehead Poetry Books,* but the work of weightier poets such as John Newlove is not exactly common coin; quotations from Purdy, Layton, or Atwood do not spring to the lips of our legislators as they engage in witty debate in the House. The wide circulation of all this *Cogswellerie* is cause for depression because, as usual, bad coin drives out good.

Poetry is no longer widely taught in high schools. Many teachers seem to feel uncomfortable with poetry, unsure of themselves. They do not themselves *read* poetry. Children reared on *Sesame Street* find poetry too demanding, gratification not sufficiently immediate. Language which flows from the literal to the metaphoric is elusive, difficult, hard to pin down and elucidate, baffling.

Trendy educators, smugly sure of the answer, have asked rhetorically: Is Milton *relevant* to our students?

(A list of what *is* relevant to an average teen-ager would make a mighty short list; it would be headed by food, sleep, and sexual intercourse — and not necessarily in that order.)

Many years ago, in what now seems a prophetic speech to the Poetry Book Society in London, T. S. Eliot said:

"I have always held firmly that a nation which ceases to produce poetry will in the long run cease to be able to enjoy and even understand the great poetry of its own past."

There is not *one* literary artist in Canada who is not supported directly or indirectly by the Canada Council. Canadians have so little regard for serious literary work that if the Canada Council were dissolved there would *be* no literature.

The art historian E. H. Gombrich in his book, *The Story of Art,* concluded:

"Artists, we trust, will always be born. But whether there will also be art depends to no small extent on ourselves, their public. By our indifference or our interest, by our prejudice or our understanding we may yet decide the issue. It is we who must see to it that the thread of tradition does not break . . . ."

The very *existence* of the Canada Council is, in many ways, an admission that Gombrich's thread is at breaking-point.

The arts in Canada have never exactly flourished. Not long ago one of our federal cabinet ministers, welcoming home a team from international competition, declared with patriotic fervour that hockey was Canada's national art form. This outrageous statement provoked only Irving Layton to public protest. The unremarked acceptance of this good minister's paean suggests why Canada remains so very much the land of Anne Murray, *Anne of Green Gables*, and Toller Cranston.

But if the situation of the arts has always been bad, it now seems, despite vast transfusions of state cash, to be getting worse. It is not only literature which languishes. Music, painting, film, architecture — the continued existence of all is precarious. Painters with major reputations would not survive without purchases by the Canada Council Art Bank. We simply do not *have* architecture. And as for Canadian music . . .

Were it *true* that we are moving from a "linear book-culture" towards some new "non-linear" cultural utopia of pictures and images, then it would be reasonable to expect a strong and popular interest in Canadian film and video. A glance at the entertainment section of a newspaper, however, suggests that the populace is wedded to naughty American movies of the *Teenage Buttocks* variety — though these are exhibited in theatres with admittedly Canadian names such as *Le Beaver*.

Where is our Bergman?

Our Fellini?

That is to ask *inappropriate* questions.

With the blessings, and indeed guidance, of the State, the Canadian film industry has been turned into a tax-haven for dentists.

What stand does our education system take against prevailing mediocrity, against the philistine values which inform Canadian life? That is, of course, a rhetorical question. Our education system professes Nutrition and Driver's Ed.

We would naturally expect teachers of English to proclaim and profess our literature. We would expect them to be its natural guardians and advocates. But quite obviously they are not. Teachers, students, schools, universities — something has gone terribly wrong.

What is that 'something'? To attempt to answer that question I must be personal and go back eighteen or nineteen years to the time I was teaching in high schools in Montreal where I wasted years of my life attempting to carry out provincial curriculum regulations which decreed that Shakespeare and Dickens be taught to children who were baffled by the Hardy Boys.

Standards, the old academic standards, were being defended against the onslaught with magnificent mindlessness. The walking wounded were shuffled off into basement remedial classes where they played with SRA Reading Labs and enjoyed colouring in the chart which recorded their alleged scientific alleged advance on literacy. All the rest, and no excuses, the long, the short, and the tall, paraded for the study of Dickens and Shakespeare.

The battle was desperate. The reluctant troops pored over Coles and Monarch Notes. Some dedicated teachers dictated *synopses* of Coles Notes. Even the Classics Comics version of *Julius Caesar* was not spurned as a study aid. The English Curriculum Consultant for the Protestant School Board of Greater Montreal, in a desperate rear-guard action, issued a 45-page mimeographed blow-by-blow account of the plot of *Great Expectations*.

And then the horde rolled over the thin red line.

After a brief period of wound-licking, most teachers seemed to give a mental shrug and subscribed to the theory that if students couldn't be beaten, they'd better be joined. This rout on the education front was symptomatic of strong social upheavals everywhere and it was not long before certain educators with true Panglossian insight perceived that this massive defeat was not a defeat at all but an overwhelming victory.

Which brings us to the Hall-Dennis Report.

But before considering *that* infamous document and its

effects, let us consider further the real nature of the war I've just described.

Now that the dust has settled, it's fairly obvious that what had been happening was roughly as follows. The curriculum in place had been one designed for an academic, university-bound minority, a minority of, at a guess, 12% of the age group. When the schools expanded to take in 70% or 80% of the age group, or more, the curriculum was not reconsidered or revised in any radical way. Mild dilution was the order of the day. The bed, in other words, was not altered to fit the sleepers, but limbs were chopped off to fit the sleepers to the bed. The resentment of the sleepers is easily understood and shared.

I do not mourn this defeat of the Old Guard. They were doggedly unintelligent, refusing to recognize that literature could not be taught to children of average ability. But more important, they did a hollow job of teaching literature to clever children. Few of them taught literature with intelligence, passion, love, and reverence.

Most teachers seemed to be staunch supporters of an authority and tradition the details and purpose of which they'd somehow forgotten — rather like the semi-civilized British after the Romans had left continuing to perform intricate and only half-remembered changing-of-the-guard procedures in front of a decaying building they didn't know how to repair.

The real, though unstated, purpose of education then was, I think, the imposition and exercise of hierarchy and authority.

I was happy to see the Bastille fall.

But in the aftermath of the war, what baby there ever had been was thrown out with the bathwater.

It was obviously deranged to inflict Shakespeare on people who were more than satisfied with *The Price Is Right* but it is equally deranged, and worse, wicked, to offer 'relevant' pap to those capable of Shakespeare. And 'offer', in the case of Ontario, is the operative word. That English could become an 'elective' subject in Ontario is indicative of the demoralization of the teaching profession and the appalling extent of its abdication of responsibility.

Which brings us back to the Hall-Dennis Report, a document whose effects betrayed a generation of Canadian schoolchildren.

Drugs, brown rice, guitars, flower power, Trudeaumania,

You're Tremendous, I'm Terrific, bizarre religious cults, primal screams, Woodstock, gay power, infant rights, the liberation of anything that moved, zen, hair, the doing of one's own thing, the letting of things hang out, vibrators, identity crises, boring goddamn people *finding themselves* all over the damn place — it's all rather embarrassing in retrospect, isn't it?

And the Hall-Dennis Report is very much of this sentimental time and tide.

(The frightening thing, of course, is that the Flower Children are now working in the New York Stock Exchange or importing cocaine by jet for the Mafia while the Hall-Dennis Report's pretty petals are caught as if in amber, institutionalized.)

I have watched speeches on the philosophy of education in Ontario performed by Dr. Dennis. I use the word 'watched' because his presentations are dominated by baroque visual aids. These pictures — The Yellow School Bus of Education, for example — are masked by sheets of brown paper and unveiled as each simple point is made. It's all rather like *Pilgrim's Progress.* The presentations pulse with energy and bonhomous showmanship. It does not take long to realize that one is being asked to stumble down to the front and sign up with the saved at a sort of secular revival meeting.

The point of the sermon seems to be that the Yellow School Bus of Education will carry us safely along The Roads of Uncertainty so long as it is driven by Compassion, Fair Play, and Love.

I do not doubt Dr. Dennis' sincerity.

After the last sermon I witnessed, preached at Beverley Elementary School in Delta, it was discovered that during the performance some doubtless disadvantaged lads from the village, the especial objects of Dr. Dennis' Compassion, had let the air out of his tires. This did much to restore my faith in human nature.

Of course, the Hall-Dennis Report is simply an attempt to find an answer to the question I've been avoiding all evening: what do we *do* with 90% or more of our school population once we've admitted that it's impossible to teach them the old academic curriculum?

I don't know the answer to that question. I believe, passionately, that the answer does *not* lie in Nutrition and Consumer Ed.

But unfortunately, the answers will probably always be matters of expediency, of politics rather than philosophy.

What concerns me as a writer — and I emphasize that — *as a writer* — is what happens to the gifted and literate minority.

When the Old Guard was defeated, many teachers seemed to lose direction and purpose; many became uncomfortable with the very idea of authority. The Hall-Dennis Report seemed to offer a way out, a new, somehow 'democratic' vision. It institutionalized the doing of one's own thing; it clothed with respectability the doctrine of different strokes for different folks.

How was it possible to say, 'Shakespeare is the world's greatest writer and you will study him'? Wasn't that a 'value judgement'? How did such a statement jibe with the Doctrine of Different Strokes? Making children happy and pleasing them seemed as important as teaching them. To not please them smacked of repression. Was it making the child *happy* to insist that there was a body of knowledge that must be mastered? And — here was the crux — *was* there, in fact, such a body of knowledge? Was Shakespeare *really* relevant in a world of computers and micro-technology? Were the activities of the ancient Romans *really* relevant in the nuclear age?

We all know how such questions were answered. Less was demanded, progressively, even of the gifted, and less was received. Translated from theory to practice, the Hall-Dennis Report meant that teachers substituted *Star Trek* for *Macbeth*. The tone of the schools became increasingly anti-intellectual. Libraries became Resource Centres. We heard more and more about such vaguely psychiatric notions as 'growth', 'self', 'fulfillment' etc. etc.

When the first of these fulfilled students graduated from high schools, the colleges and universities pandered too. They had to. They had sections to fill, *per capita* grants to snare. Soon the universities were offering courses *in remedial English*. Think about that. And now think about it again. Mature Students were welcomed; the academic requirements for a Mature Student were that he or she be over nineteen. The coffers clinked with coin. Courses in literary basket-weaving abounded. At one institution of Higher Learning at which I was employed a course was offered in Androgyny; in California, there are now, I understand, Professors of Thanatology. Do they study, I wonder, *The*

Loved One? Registration weeks at our universities turned into sleazy bazaars where the students picked over the increasingly shoddy goods on display.

That is history.

What of the future?

Before going on to write prescriptions, I must stress again that I am talking as a writer who feels that he is living in a society which, despite the proliferation of regional theatres and Awards of $50,000 for novels about stern ladies running pig farms, is on the verge of cultural collapse. Some of you may feel that I have been unfair, perhaps even totally prejudiced, in my evaluation of the part that the educational system has played in our current shame. I can only ask you to reflect on the statistics I gave you earlier.

If you can dispute them, I'd be delighted.

Others among you may be wondering what all the fuss is about; you may hold the view I've often heard expressed in staff rooms and faculty clubs: Surely Shakespeare's better than Irving Layton? This is a critical estimate with which even Irving Layton might agree. But what underlies the comment, of course, is the charge that Canadian writing just isn't good enough.

It is unfortunately true that most Canadian writing up until about 1950 is rubbish. It is also true and unfortunate that the universities have seized on this *dreck* and unleashed upon it some of their dreariest minds. It is a case of like calling unto like. Thus unspeakable poets who might warrant a footnote are pumped up into swollen significance; dreary scriveners like Frederick Philip Grove are invested with such honours as 'father of the Canadian novel'. Mordecai Richler was closer to the mark when he described Grove as 'a good speller'.

What has happened *since* 1950 is, however, a different story. Many of our writers are as good as the best in the United States and England. A partial list might include: Margaret Laurence, Margaret Atwood, Hugh Hood, Alice Munro, John Newlove, Irving Layton, Mordecai Richler, Clark Blaise, Leon Rooke, Mavis Gallant, Ethel Wilson, Norman Levine — the list is long and vital. And there are many talented younger writers struggling to keep alive and warm in an inhospitable climate.

The charge that Canadian writing 'isn't good enough' is a charge usually made from a position of entrenched ignorance.

What can we do, then, about this crisis?

What, specifically, can teachers do?

It would be easy to offer patchwork solutions. Buy the occasional book. Teach more CanLit courses. Support literary magazines through school libraries. Take a starving writer out to dinner. But these are not real solutions and would change nothing. Such measures as these are rather like putting a quarter in an Oxfam box in the hope of ameliorating mass starvation in Africa.

The facts that face us are simple. Many teachers teach courses in Canadian literature. Larger numbers of students take these courses. Yet writers do not seem able to reach an audience of more than 1500. We are forced to the conclusion that there is no carry-over; the course finished and the credit secured, the students revert to *The Dukes of Hazard*.

Such widespread and profound lack of impact surely requires some explanation. What accounts for this massive failure?

It is most logical to start at the top with the universities and the training of teachers, with the educators who formulate the theories that teachers must implement. Education in Ontario, the Ministry proudly proclaims in all its brochures, is 'child-centered'. Right there in the opening line is the most obvious explanation of our problems. Education should not be 'child-centred'; it should be subject-centred. Children should be brought to our subject; we should not court the child.

Who would wish to be operated on by a surgeon whose medical training had been 'doctor-centred'? Who would wish to drive across a bridge built by an engineer who was ever so creative?

There *are* bodies of knowledge which have taken us thousands of years to build. Some children will add to those bodies of knowledge, perhaps totally transform them, but they won't do so until they've mastered what past generations have built. To be 'child-centred' is to believe in the daily re-invention of the wheel.

Departments of Education and Training Colleges teach young teachers everything but the one thing they should be taught. All over North America, teacher education has commonly been seen for many years, and not unfairly, as mickey mousery necessary to get a work-permit. The universities themselves have lowered their standards under the pressure of the grant system and the degrees they confer have become debased coinage.

Failure is nearly unknown.

(The last time I failed a university student — he had written, for reasons unknown, a lengthy comparison of the work of Margaret Laurence and Elton John — I had to appear before the Student Ombudsman and a panel of three of my teaching colleagues to justify this radical act.)

Teachers enter the profession bulging with knowledge of child psychology and other such buffoonery but ill-informed about their subject. Some can't spell. Few can write crisp English. And how many of them *love books*?

We will not have good teachers until we have teachers who love their subject, who reverence its tradition, who revel in what Auden called 'dazzling displays of concinnity and elegance', teachers who live for language. Our best students will not catch fire until their obdurate flint meets the steel of the Word.

The answer is that simple.

But it is not simply a matter of better pedagogical preparation. Such love as I speak of is a matter of the whole man. It cannot be imparted in a three-credit course. It is the sum of what a man or woman *is*. It should be obvious to all of us by now that culture cannot be legislated. Rock cannot be made to flower by decree. Culture is a living thing, something that grows. It is the sum of many disparate lives. It is the slow accumulation of endless acts of faith and love.

I did not refer earlier to our cabinet minister's remarks about hockey merely to indulge in what a friend of mine calls "Canuck-bashing" nor to pillory the minister in question — the Canadian cabinet does not hold a monopoly on foolishness — but because the minister's remarks were more germane than he realized. There are good reasons why Canada produces fine hockey players. For each hockey player who achieves national fame, there are thousands of boys who live and breathe the game, who watch every match, who pore over the hockey cards in bubble gum packets, who play passionately and with burning ambition in streets and alleys until the light fails. And there are mothers and fathers who sanction and foster this ambition, forcing themselves out of bed to drive these boys to practices in the morning dark, forcing themselves out at night to coach and cheer the little leagues.

A great hockey player emerges from *a hockey world*.

All Canadians understand this yet seem puzzled that after pouring good public money down the funnel of the Canada Council they don't seem to be getting Picasso out of the other end.

The simple truth is that just as hockey players are produced from a hockey world, Canadian artists will be, in part, a product of a great Canadian public, a public which is informed, critical, and passionate. Good writing will come from a culture in which native readers, teachers, and students read native writers simply because it is the *normal thing* to read one's own literature.

It is at present rather difficult to read a Canadian book without feeling faintly *virtuous*. Our present "culture" is a subsidized and legislated culture; it must become, however narrowly, a possession of real people.

I have been speaking of 'faith' and 'love'. How does my sermon differ, then, from that of Dr. Dennis? In *my* sermon, love is made of sterner stuff; it is both lavished and *demanded*. Determination is not necessarily rewarded. Fair Play is irrelevant. Unto everyone that hath shall, unfairly, undemocratically, be given. And I can assure you that your daily acts of faith will be betrayed, your love and devotion spurned.

The idea of a culture, then, does not rest with legislatures, commissions, White Papers, and massive infusions of State cash, but with *you*, with each one of you loving and having faith in something larger and profounder than yourselves. I do not mean that we should become earnest and humourless fanatics. I mean that we should *live* what in our professional lives we profess.

And what, precisely, does *that* mean?

It means that literary taste cannot be separated from the minute and endless activities of our daily lives. What I am trying to say sounds very simple and is not. We read, we understand, we teach what we are. Every time we choose white sliced as opposed to bread, every time we make do with an ugly cup or plate or knife or fork, every time we ignore or are blind to ugliness in our rooms and furnishings, our senses atrophy further and we weaken our ability to share in the visions of those who see more clearly than we do. Every time we accept the convenience of the shoddy, the seeming inevitability of the vulgar, the less able we are to stand up against the values of the market place. If we drink coffee in styrofoam cups from machines, is it not likely that this, and an accumulation of such acts, progressively blunts us? If we do not protest against reconstituted potatoes or frozen french fries, is it really likely that we will protest against imprecise and incorrect language in our newspapers and on the CBC? Would Evelyn Waugh have washed his hair with a shampoo called *Gee, Your Hair Smells Terrific?*

We teach what we are.

I must stress the absolute inevitability of opposition and alienation. Canada offers you no choice. We have created a society so vulgar that you cannot be happily of this world and at the same time a good teacher. All literature now is subversive. All literature subverts with its passionate craft the very bases of our society. Read the signs.

Big Bucks.

Top Dollar.

A good teacher not only teaches literature — he *celebrates* literature. The good teacher is less likely, then, to be sitting in the Yellow School Bus of Education than sprawled in ambush with the driver in his sights. This, then, in conclusion, is a call to arms. You must leave the fat city, the lush meadows of the Park Plaza, and join the resistance in the hills.

Be prepared for a long fight.

Telling Tales

MONTREAL STORY TELLERS — a group made up of myself, Clark Blaise, Ray Fraser, Hugh Hood, and Ray Smith, and formed to give public readings — was not a literary 'movement'. The word 'movement' implies common aims, excited talk, a manifesto scrawled on menus. *Montreal Story Tellers* was united only in the base desire for emolument. At least, that's true of the beginning.

We did talk a lot among ourselves about the educational virtues of our activities, about snaring a new generation of readers, about charging the batteries of the teachers themselves. In the period of questions and answers which followed readings we did promote Canadian writers and writing with missionary zeal. But we all had more than a passing interest in used bills of small denomination.

(Ray Smith, whose father was the manager of a bank, kept the accounts. These accounts were kept in a very *severe* book and were professionally incomprehensible. Ray worried about these accounts. The rest of us could not have cared less. Ray worried about reporting sums earned to the tax-gatherers. The rest of us felt he was being overly particular. Hugh's position was that such sums *were not taxable* — an example of the radical simplicity and profundity of much of Hugh's thought. In essence, his theory, with which I was and am in total agreement, was that *any* sum he was paid for reading, ten or ten thousand dollars, was an honorarium, a mere token, a formal gesture of gratitude, because his reading was beyond price. Honoraria could not rationally be considered as income. Therefore honoraria were not taxable. An argument which Hugh, to quote Hugh quoting W. C. Fields, often said would be found to hold water.)

The most common questions we were asked were, 'How much do you earn?' and 'Who do you write for?' This latter was not an untutored groping towards such a figment as V. Woolf's 'Common Reader' but meant exactly what it said. It meant: 'Which company pays you to write? *The Reader's Digest? Maclean's?*' Such questions led to explanations of sales and royalties, returns and remainders. When the children grasped that we earned from stories less than they did from paper-routes or baby-sitting, they politely did their best to disguise their conviction that we were potty.

After twenty sessions or so of answering the same question, our advocacy of Truth, Beauty, The Joy of Art, etc. sounded a bit thin even to us.

But it was pleasing and sustaining simply to be together. Writing is a necessarily lonely occupation but writing in Canada approximates solitary confinement. I'm convinced that the lack of audience, the lack of response, accounts for the slow rate of composition of so many Canadian writers and their early silencing.

Together, sustained by each other, we could make light of the fact that no large bookstore in Montreal carried our books. We could make light of the fact that the paperback reissues of *A North American Education* and *Tribal Justice* were shelved in Classics Book Shop under 'Education' and 'Anthropology'. We could make light of the fact that no university in Montreal expressed the faintest interest in engaging us to read; that the *doyen* of Montreal literary journalists, John Richmond of the Montreal *Star*, refused to acknowledge our existence.

Well, he said, when Hugh once remonstrated, *you never invite me round to crack a bottle of sherry, do you, dear boy?*

Of course, this 'sustaining' was never articulated; it expressed itself in general hilarity. We never discussed literature or technique. We all had very high standards of craftsmanship and respected each other's craft but we did not offer criticism and wouldn't have accepted it. I think it was Thurber who said that in the literary world no one sits at anyone's feet unless they've been knocked there. Most of our journeys to and from readings were taken up with Hugh and Clark swapping baseball trivia or with Hugh's photographic horrible memory unwinding paragraphs from Chandler or Wodehouse; our task was to identify which books they came from. Ray and Ray often traded hints and wrinkles about home-brewing and bottling, sediment problems. Ray Smith, a superb cook, might reveal the latest round in his lengthy controversy with a cooking expert on the CBC about the use of cheddar cheese in the manufacture of Welsh Rarebit. Ray claimed that with all *advertised* methods, cheddar went funny. Beer came into it somewhere. It usually did. Clark often detailed yet another financial reversal. On the day he told us his house had just burned down, we all, I think, accepted the news as somehow unexciting and *inevitable*. What I talked about, I can't remember. I really did try to place Hugh's quotations.

"Shall I give you a clue?"

"Yes."

"It's *before* 1935."

If one of us did comment on a compatriot's work, Ray Smith would attempt to guide us back to baseball or the great P. G. by saying, "I don't read books by Canadian writers". This plonking statement was not merely an attempt to end unwelcome topics; it was also true. Literary shop-talk of any kind seemed to cause him great distress. In this, he was much like Professor Alec Lucas of McGill who endeared himself to me one evening at a book-launching for a young poet. Free drink flowed. People were chatting of this and that. Waiters circulated with gratifying frequency. Then another professor called for silence and proposed that the young man read to us from his book. Professor Lucas said to me in a very loud and *petulant* voice,

"They always have to *spoil* these occasions."

I've said that we all had high standards of craftsmanship. I should perhaps change that statement. We all liked Ray Fraser personally, of course, but perhaps only Hugh was a devotee of Ray's fiction.

Ray's stories were less stories than anecdotes or tales. They were typed on yellow newsprint and heavily influenced in style and subject matter by his former employment at the tabloid *Midnight*. Most of these yarns seemed to feature massive inso-briety, murder, incest, mutilation, rape, anal crime, and genital abnormality.

Once when we were reading at the University of New Brunswick in Fredericton, Ray managed to clear a fair part of a large auditorium with a scabrous *conte* entitled "Spanish Jack" which detailed the aftermath of a Maritime Golden Ager's ingestion of cantharides. Or perhaps I've got it wrong. Perhaps it was the one about the underprivileged Maritimer in a knocking-shop who couldn't get it up. In memory, they tend to merge.

By the time he was but three sentences in, four nuns left in a marked manner.

The lay folk left later.

(Ray published a selection of these yarns in a book called *The Black Horse Tavern*. My feathers were considerably ruffled when Dennis Duffy of all people reviewed the book and perversely declared it to be the best collection of stories since *The Lady Who Sold Furniture*.)

Ray Smith was impressed by a certain *carefree* quality in Fraser's sentences and after profound inebriated thought produced the following which he claimed was quintessential Fraser:

"She looked like an old bag of forty — which she was, by Christ!"

(The full effect requires that the sentence be read with a very long pause at the dash and with an emphasis on 'was' and stronger emphasis and gravelly tone on the 'by Christ!')

Ray had large numbers of these yellow stories which he stuffed into his army-surplus knapsack as he left the house. He read them unedited and sometimes with pages missing. Nothing fazed him. To sustain himself he always brought with him a mickey of brandy which was swigged in the wings. He always bought the cheapest brandy he could find. Amazing brandy. Brandy from countries one would not associate with the grape. Such as Patagonia. He often read last and was usually flushed.

I had urged Ray to clean these stories up because in some of the Catholic schools the bad language was not happily received. I did not want our agreement with the Catholic School Commission cancelled. We had a minor row on the subject; he promised that the next week his story would be as the driven snow.

The next week was a rushed affair. Hugh picked everyone up at 1 p.m. Ray was still in bed when we arrived. He threw on his clothes, grabbed up his knapsack. We rushed to the school. "No smut!" we reminded him before he went on stage. But in his haste he had grabbed up yet another impure tale.

He got himself launched into the matter and then found himself in a passage of abusive dialogue between two of his disgusting Maritime low-lifes. Backstage, we listened with great uneasiness as the dialogue wound up to one of the characters saying:

"By Christ! Someone ought to string the son of a whore up by his . . ."

66

At this point, Fraser, whose lips were already forming the word 'balls', remembered. He gazed out over the sea of Catholic girlhood, paralyzed.

The silence went on and on.

And on.

Suddenly, and triumphantly, he said, *"Thumbs!"*

I once heard Clark introduce one of his own readings by saying rather sadly that he was being paid more for reading aloud for one hour than he received in royalties in a year. It's sometimes impossible not to feel angry about this. We all of us would have preferred to sit at home and receive royalties. We would have preferred readers to listeners. Readers work harder and stand a chance of getting more. But as the principal of a school in which I once worked used to murmur when it was reported to him that children had again emptied their free milk into the grand piano, "We live in an imperfect world".

None of us was ever seduced, so far as I know, by the idea of performance. We all realized that writing and performing were entirely distinct activities and that, for us, writing was the sterner and more valuable task. My own work and Clark's lent itself most naturally to performance. Hugh's prose — certainly from his later novels but also in some of the stories — tends to be too complex to be grasped at a reading. The same is true of Clark's prose, of course, or mine, but our subtleties are of a different kind from Hugh's; we seem to be far more transparent. There are various reasons for this: much of Clark's work is in the first person and this creates an immediate intimacy; first-person writing seems to the unwary or unskilled listener less 'literary', the choice of a first-person narrator dictating a relatively simple syntax and vocabulary. In my own case, unskilled listeners probably fail to understand how complex and *literary* the simplicity is — particularly in dialogue. Behind the 'naturalness' of my dialogue, for which I've sometimes been commended, are echoes of such naturalistic writers as P. G., Firbank, Waugh, and Amis.

(The complexity of 'simplicity' is rarely grasped. A very crafty poet like John Newlove, for example, is generally seen as 'simple' which is both true and very much not true — a misunderstanding that won't be cured until we've managed to teach people to experience the 'how' of a work instead of grubbing

67

about for an unfindable 'what'. An understanding which will occur, if the experience of my teaching career is anything to go by, at about the same time that pigs take to the air.)

My years with *Montreal Story Tellers* persuaded me that there is a strong, though not obvious, connection between a writer's conversational and literary style. An obvious example — a very small part of Hugh's literary complexity is the *formality* of his syntax, a formality which is mirrored in his speech. I suspect that a writer's literary range and style, the genres in which he is likely to succeed or fail, are intimately connected with the styles and patterns of his conversation.

Reading to a responsive audience is a pleasure for me. Reading to an *audience* isn't bad either; I recently supported Eastern Ontario Library Week by reading at the Brockville Public Library to an audience of the Chief Librarian, the Assistant Librarian, and my wife. And *she'd* heard it before.

There are particular reasons why my own work reads well — or *should* read well. I was at home very early in life with the idea of performance and with the handling of rhetoric because I listened every Sunday to two of my father's sermons. If he happened to be preaching elsewhere, I had the rare pleasure of hearing two of someone else's. And these were not your average Anglican chat but full-blown, non-conformist, three-quarters-of-an-hour jobs with plenty of side on the ball. I don't think I'm exaggerating or distorting when I say that even as a small child I developed a grasp of rhetorical structures.

When I was five or six, it was feared that my older brother's eyesight was failing. My mother, to spare his eyes, used to read his homework aloud him. I can remember, vastly improbable as it sounds, being absolutely ravished by Shakespeare, literally felled by Malvolio. Another great source of pleasure at the time was *Toytown*, a serial for children on the BBC I'm sure I drew no distinctions between Malvolio and Larry the Lamb. Which on reflection is probably a good thing.

It was only while writing this essay that I realized how large a part radio and the spoken word played in forming the way I write and wish to write. When I was a child, the radio was switched on *to be listened to*. I cannot understand how it is possible to turn on radios for companionable noise and not hear what the horrid voices are talking about. If I catch even seconds of Don

Harron's voice before the (usually ill-read) news, it causes me almost unbearable anguish. The effect upon me of Barbara Frum is even more marked. To this day, I hear *everything* and increasingly envy those who don't.

I used to listen to many of the BBC programmes for children, the *William* stories, stories about Norman and Henry Bones, Boy Detectives, Dick Barton — Special Agent, and a host of others now largely forgotten. As I grew older, I listened to all the fine comedy programmes which culminated in the most entrancing radio programme ever produced — *The Goon Show*. The Goons created worlds in which I have never ceased to believe and in Major Bloodnok a character in that long tradition of military realists that you can stack up against Falstaff any day of the week.

I am always deeply affected by his shaken cry,

"No more curried eggs for me!"

Concurrent with the Goons, lesser but still adored performers lifted up my heart — Frankie Howerd and the simperingly lewd Benny Hill. Frankie Howerd's announcement to a female travel agent that he has come in to see her brochures, her *tours*, so appealed to me that I pinched it for *General Ludd*.

I was a devotee of splendidly coarse reviews in the theatre starring such stalwarts as 'Professor' Jimmy Edwards, Tony Hancock, and Harry Secombe, and of the great tradition of low farce.

On the BBC Third Programme in the fifties there were frequent plays, usually commissioned, by writers like N. F. Simpson, Giles Cooper, Harold Pinter, and Samuel Beckett. I can still remember coming home from school one evening and settling down to listen to a play by a playwright unknown to me then and being wrapped in increasing horror and delight. The actor was, I believe, Jack McGowran. The play was *All That Fall*.

And I'm afraid age hasn't cured me.

One of my treasured possessions is a record of the last music hall performance of the great Max Miller — "The Cheekie Chappie", as he was billed. I've listened to it countless times and never cease to marvel at the control he exercised over audiences. I sent a copy of it to John Mills knowing that it would tug at ancestral memory and he wrote back reminding me of a line Maxie had perpetrated during a live BBC broadcast — a jest about meeting a lady on a narrow mountain ledge and not knowing whether to block her passage or toss himself off.

But that gives nothing of the full wonders of the *voice*.

I listened to all this stuff intently and intensely, studied it almost, and I realize now that it formed one important strand in my sense of accent and timing, of the voice as instrument. Reading and performance, then, is no trial for me. More important, it's no violation of my own work. When I'm writing, I'm always *listening* to what I'm doing. If it doesn't work aloud, I always change it because if it doesn't work aloud it doesn't work at all.

(One of the most perfect pieces of *voice* I've ever managed, a chunk I'm quite proud of, is the conversation between Jim Wells and Mr. Bhardwaj in Chapter Eleven of *General Ludd* — classy stuff, I thought, and memorable, though possibly caviar for the general as reviewers seem to have concentrated on the fancied sociological and political import of the tome.)

I have often changed what I had previously considered finished stories after a public reading. In fact, I use readings for just this purpose. I listen to myself, listen to the rhythms, and as I read make mental notes of where there's dead wood, awkwardnesses, where the timing is a beat or two off. I don't derive this information from the reaction of the audience — that would be perilous. The flow of adrenalin during a performance seems to stimulate an innate sense of what is correct.

It's impossible for me to tell the unvarnished truth about the members of *Montreal Story Tellers* as readers, as performers, because the truth is doubtless enhanced by a heavy patina of love and affection. I think we were all damn good and good as a group.

Ray Smith tended to be rather nervous and rigid when he started and if he fluffed lines often apologized and started over. As he continued, he usually relaxed considerably adding gesture and large movement. His rendition of "A Cynical Tale" from *Cape Breton Is the Thought-Control Centre of Canada* was often very funny; there was the added pleasure of incongruity in watching arch suggestions of the feminine or homosexual conveyed by such a very huge man. Ray was a bit defeated at the beginning by the arcane nature of some of the stories in *Cape Breton*; they were not exactly what you might call a good read. This was not particularly surprising as the impulse behind them was almost "anti-story". Ray and I used to read together from the second section of his story "Peril" in an effort to jazz things up. Ray read all the narration and the part of Peril while I boomed the part of G. K. Chesterton.

(I do not mean to imply that Ray's work in *Cape Breton* was not good; I'm merely saying that I wouldn't have chosen it as a natural to read to high school students. Or college students, come to that. "Peril" is a very funny story and moves in its final section into a delicate and affecting lyricism. It is also a very *odd* story. I also happen to think that it's among the best stories ever written in Canada.)

Later, when Ray was working on *Lord Nelson Tavern*, the nature of the material gave him greater scope and he was able to let himself go on monologues and more 'realistic' dialogue. These lively passages were usually in the *voice* of other people. It was always my impression *listening* to Ray that he had not worked through to an *authorial* voice with which he was entirely comfortable.

Clark's stories ran on wheels, as it were; Clark gave the impression that he was merely the almost invisible track on which they ran. The stories are so beautifully crafted and balanced in terms of their rhetoric that Clark seemed almost to disappear behind them. This was, of course, an illusion. Clark was never openly dramatic, never given to gesture, but he read fluently and *urgently* and with a fierce grip on the audience which tightened relentlessly. It was rather like watching an oddly silent pressure-cooker which you knew was capable of taking the roof off at any moment. This feeling of *contained* power, typical of Clark's performing style, was also somehow connected with Clark's temperament. I've never seen Clark not in control of himself but I'd pay large sums of money not to be there if or when.

Clark is an excellent mimic and it was amazing when in those few stories which contain dialogue, voices other than the narrating voice flashed out. It was rather like lightning against a heavy sky, to hear Southern "cracker" voices or the precise imprecisions of East Indian English. At such times, Clark was riotously funny; I'm thinking fondly of his reading the Princess Hi Yalla section in "A North American Education".

(I remember asking Clark once why he didn't use dialogue more often and I *think* he said that dialogue was too easy to write. This may be true. For him. Or it may not. I always got the impression that Clark quite literally *relaxed* when speaking in voices other than his "own" and I sometimes felt that this relaxation frightened him.)

Ray Fraser's style and manner was confused and bumbling. One was always aware that Ray was *reading* something — not least because he often lost his place. If he provoked laughter, he would laugh himself and then find his place again, blushing, pushing his glasses higher with his thumb, a modest and nervous gesture. Ray sometimes gave the impression that he was as surprised as the audience at the way the events in the story were turning out — and this may well have been true.

Hugh Hood's reading style was again related to his matter. I've heard him read quite wildly on such stories as "Whos Paying For This Call" but that, like the story, was untypical. Hugh's normal reading style gave the impression, as do many of the stories, of being something like *heightened conversation*. There was an intimacy and familiarity about Hugh's reading — as though you too were very intelligent and he wished to share with you an interesting experience. This did not preclude emphasis and shading in delivery, of course, but the stance is rhetorically low-key. His style was so 'personal' and persuasive, so much someone 'talking', that I'm sure most listeners were unaware of the tropes being paraded in front of them.

Hugh did have one tremendous fault as a reader which worked against the willing suspension of disbelief. When I first heard him do it, I cringed. Later, I found it endearing. Now, my love for him is such that I would feel deprived if he read without indulging this mild eccentricity.

Hugh would stop in the middle of a paragraph, sometimes in the middle of a sentence, and start to chuckle at some rediscovered felicity. Sometimes he would shake his head as if amazed that he had got off such a perfect shot. He would say,

"You know, that's a *honey* of a sentence! I think I'll read that again."

And did.

Audiences didn't seem to find this particularly surprising but possibly because they thought we were all bloody weird anyway.

Of my own reading, I can't say much. Hugh's remarks on his own work while reading it suggest tremendous involvement in what he was doing, suggest almost an obliviousness of audience. When I read, I am fairly coldly concerned with manipulation of the audience. I am moving them to laughter or a moist eye but remain unmoved myself. From the intensity of their laughter or tension I do receive a current which enables me to pour it on the more — it's difficult to read powerfully to an audience of three — but I'm always fully aware that *I* am 'playing' *them*. It's an exhausting business because, although you're receiving current, you're giving out a hell of a lot more than you receive.

Unlike writing, the rewards are immediate, which explains why writers are attracted to the idea of reading their work. But the rewards are also ephemeral and, not being professional actors, we were all aware, I think, of some such image as seals being thrown gobbets of herring after launching themselves through hoops.

To have written something beautifully is its own reward but it also exists permanently on the page. I can scarcely comprehend the life of a professional actor. It must be rather like that of an addict needing daily, and larger, doses. I'm grateful to actors for all the pleasure they've given me and for what I've learned from them but I'm even more grateful I didn't become one. A writer, writing, is in some sort of relationship of equality with an ideal audience. I suspect that an actor's life is, paradoxically, more lonely than a writer's and that it is, essentially, masturbatory; I suspect that a good actor's relationship with an audience is tinged in some complicated way with contempt.

Most of the readings by *Montreal Story Tellers*, apart from a relatively small number in universities, CEGEPs, and off-island Protestant schools, took place in schools under the jurisdiction of the Montreal Catholic School Commission. One of Hugh's former students at the University of Montreal happened to be the English Coordinator for the Commission and so was disposed to be helpful.

We were, of course, very interested in reading in the schools administered by the Protestant School Board of Greater Montreal but the Protestant Board had a very Protestant mistrust of the idea of parting with money — especially for the purpose of encouraging the profitless enjoyment of literature. I had worked for the PSBGM for some years and knew the personnel quite well. The Consultant in English with whom I had enjoyed a very friendly relationship, Charles Rittenhouse, had recently retired and had been replaced by a Welsh person. Hugh and I arranged to go to the Board offices on Fielding Avenue in Montreal to further press the case for Art, Beauty, and Truth, as telephonic communication had merely resulted in a lot of devious Welsh evasion. This visit ended in our both being banned for life from the Board offices and all schools and messuages under its jurisdiction.

Hugh is, by and large, a gentle, optimistic, cheerful character. He has many marked opinions which he is at all times more than willing to expound but always in a rational and compassionate spirit. (I remember driving with him and my wife from Delta to Toronto. As we left the house in Delta my wife asked him why he didn't buckle his seat-belt. The answer, taking in a comprehensive survey through the ages of the doctrines of Free Will, Salvation, Law, and The Social Contract, lasted until we were approaching Oshawa. My wife often recalls this answer and now, when Hugh is visiting, visibly hesitates before asking him if he would like salt . . . pepper?)

Hugh's cheerfulness and optimism must take its toll, however, because very infrequently he explodes into awe-inspiring rage. So it was that afternoon at the offices of the Protestant School Board of Greater Montreal.

Montreal at that time lived in fear of FLQ bombs and the PSBGM had installed in the foyer of their headquarters an armed guard who refused to let us enter until we had identified ourselves and announced the nature of our business. His request was rather like poking a stick into an innocent-looking hole and being forced to run for one's life in front of an advancing wall of white-hot magma.

Hugh refused to identify himself. He refused to let *me* identify myself. He demanded to know the name of the guard. Of the receptionist. Of the switchboard girl. He wrote their names down in his note-book. By this time, covert phone-calls were being made. The Welsh person arrived. The mounting uproar roused ancient functionaries from their slumbers in the Boardroom. The Comptroller came and gawked. Down in their private elevator came Directors of Personnel and Consultants.

74

Hugh, pinched of nostril and white with rage, was in full spate, reminding them, very reasonably in my opinion, that the schools they administered were paid for by *his* taxes; that all of them were *his* servants, not he theirs; that the building, perhaps more than any other, was a *public* building.

These politically unexceptionable remarks were followed by statements of a slightly more disputatious nature about the history and course of English-French relations, the part played by the Board in fostering and maintaining these social and political schisms, the accountability of the Board, the obvious political end to which their blind and high-handed attitudes would inevitably bring them. It was at about this point that the banning took place.

I must admit that there were some subsequent half-hearted gestures on their part towards reconciliation but these were curtly refused. It was a pity to have killed the Protestant Goose but we were in no mood then, or, come to that, now, to be fucked about by administrators or Welshmen.

Some of the readings we did stay more firmly in the mind than others. In one Catholic school we read in a sub-basement room which was festooned with lagged steam-pipes to a group of young slatterns — a Practical Class, I suspect, or a sorority rudely ripped from Domestic Science to form an audience. Their remarks about Clark's beard, Ray's size and probable endowment, and their projection of a contained but heightened sense of merriment filled me with foreboding. Was this, I asked myself, a natural audience for "Getting to Williamstown"? My fears were soon realized. As the outer limits of their attention span were reached, some three minutes into the reading, they deliberately began to fall off their chairs.

At another inner-city school — a nice euphemism, that — we were greeted by the principal, a large slab of a man whose ramrod bearing and aura suggested reflex violence, a sort of West Point General of a principal. His unsmiling face was marked from eye to chin by a purple scar. Those students we saw on our march to the auditorium seemed unnervingly quiet and self-effacing. The audience was unnaturally still and silent. The *feel* of the hall reminded me of those silent, panning shots in the pre-riot cafeteria in San Quentin. The teachers, all male, stood sentry in the aisles gazing at their charges. I would not go so far as to say that all the teachers were Christian Brothers but they were in the Christian Brothers class.

The reading was desperate from the start. We read our hearts out. We basely angled for laughs but got not a titter. It was like reading in a morgue. Even Ray Fraser's tale, yet another ill-judged offering, did not cause them to break ranks.

At the close of the ghastly proceedings, the principal expressed his thanks and invited the audience to express their appreciation. The applause sounded as if it were under water. The students were then marched out.

"Gentlemen," said the principal, "you will be so good as to follow me."

On the echoing march to the Office, I felt frankly nervous; I imagined Ray Fraser being held down by Christian Brothers and having his mouth washed out with soap and water. And for the rest of us, if we were lucky, a general duffing up. . .

The Office was dominated by a massive steel safe. Chairs were brought in by a muscular man. Not a word had been spoken. The principal moved to the safe, turned wheels, heaved open the door. We stared. Inside were many bottles.

"Gentlemen," he said. "What is your pleasure?"

But not all our readings, of course, were so bizarre. The most successful ones were done for Doug Rollins at Rosemere High School and, later, at Dawson College. Doug Rollins, an old friend and superb teacher, provided audiences which had been prepared. They had read some of our work and had absorbed from Doug some ideas about the story form. They were also fired by his enthusiasm. The comparative sophistication of their questions after readings was remarkable.

It's difficult to know what sort of educational impact MST made. At the time we were all aware, I think, of the missionary nature of the readings. To read Canadian matter and talk of Canadian concerns was then rather like carrying the Word to people who ate grubs and worshipped aeroplanes. One of our strengths was that we gave children the opportunity to hear and talk to living writers, creatures heretofore known only as names in italic on the contents page of an anthology or text. We appeared before them warts and all. And we talked, insistently, of being writers *in Canada*. I think this was valuable.

(I felt much the same way about the text book I'd edited at

about the same time — a book called *Sixteen by Twelve*. Writers were presented by means of photographs, brief biographies, and a chatty commentary to accompany the stories. It didn't really matter if the commentary were too difficult or even inaccurate and misleading; what mattered was the expression and impact of personality.)

The problem, though, was to wean the children from this immediately attractive stuff — from the holiday aspects of a reading, from the comedy of five grown men fooling about for their benefit — and to get them chomping on solid food, the words on the page. Personality only goes so far. We can't know how successful we were in this but we can make informed and gloomy guesses.

(So far as *I* can see, still nothing much has changed. In spite of all the nationalist furore, the founding of the Writers' Union, and the proliferation of Canada Days in schools, Canadian writing is still foreign to Canada. More to the point, perhaps, *writing* is foreign to Canada.

The educational world grinds on like the mills of God. For how many more decades, one wonders, will Canadian children have the moral and technical crudities of Hugh Garner imposed upon them? The first story I ever wrote is now beginning to be used in text books. It will still be "in use" (and I'm afraid that's *exactly* what I mean) when I'm a toothless old fart mumbling into my nightly mug of warm milk. And young writers will be raging against the weathered monoliths that stand in their way.

I apologize in advance.

My book *Sixteen by Twelve* marches on — far too successfully. I'm afraid it will still be in use in twenty years. I put the thing together in 1969. When I did so, it was, I believe, the *only* vaguely contemporary gathering of stories for schools. A number of charmers have demanded to know how I, an ex-Brit and effete limejuicer, had the nerve to compile a book of Canadian stories for schools. My innate good manners have always prevented me from explaining in corrosive detail.)

Towards the end, MST was beginning to pall. The idea of being travelling clowns confident of being able to manipulate laughs held little appeal for any of us. We were writers. Serious people. We wanted to write serious stuff. I always had before me the vision of writing stuff of the same calibre as P. G.'s *The Mating Season*, a book to which I often turn for comfort.

(There's nothing better for a dark night of the soul than Bertie Wooster pretending to be Gussie Finknottle coaching Esmond Haddock in a souped-up version of the hunting song that Esmond is to sing at the King's Deverill Village Concert.)

We had read. We had preached and proselytized. But the literary landscape had not changed. We remained prophets without honour. The earth had not moved.

But if we were not especially effective in our Mission to the Heathen, we did have an educational impact on each other. I must qualify that immediately. I cannot speak for anyone else in MST. I can say, however, that I was most definitely influenced by others in the group. What I learned is not easy to define. Listening to someone's story for the tenth (boring) time, the pieces in my own kaleidoscope would suddenly jink into a slightly different pattern.

Ray Smith's comments on and typical aggression towards the traditional story form raised red warning lights for me; he directed my attention towards dangers I'd never really seen. He forced me into more critical reading. I'd always felt that much 'experimental' writing was rather like farting Annie Laurie through a keyhole though not as demanding. The expertise was obvious, if it were well done, but the emotional power was lacking. Intimate acquaintance with Ray's story "Peril" skinned my eyeballs, as the necromancer in the first part of "Peril" says, quoting Gulley Jimson. Again.

Ray probably isn't aware of his influence on me — possibly because it's a largely negative one. Ray prevented me from perpetrating yet more gauche stories of sensitive youth. Ray has a thing about sensitive youth. Show Ray a sensitive youth in literature or life and he will don his leather coat and stride towards the Royal Pub on Guy Street, muttering.

(An example of the literary Ray at his most aggressive is the dour farce "Symbols in Agony" — a tale that dismembers Ray's vision of The Canadian Story. I remember his telling me once that his editor, Dennis Lee, had somehow managed to read the story without quite grasping that its intention was comic.)

Hugh's work reassured me of the *respectability* of writing openly about a moral world — and of writing openly. I don't mean by this anything so crude as that I saw Hugh merely as a moral influence. I mean something much more complicated.

My early writing had been constricted by rather strange notions of fictional chastity stemming from the doctrine of *Don't Tell: Show* carried to obsessively virginal lengths. Hugh offered me an example of how to relax my own style, of how to become less clenched. I didn't relax *in Hugh's manner* but that I managed to accept the possibility of relaxation is largely owing to his influence. His taste and erudition helped me get away from the conscious and precious effects of Imagism whose precepts informed, ineptly, my early prose efforts. The search for the old *mot* and my consciousness of the strictures of Hulme and Pound had induced literary constipation. I can't really remember now what it was I was attempting — probably something like the technique of a five-line H. D. lyric transferred to a 3000-word story but muddied by Hemingway mannerisms and totally contradicted by gobs of Dylan Thomas. Hugh's opinions and example were like a massive draught of laxative. Though it took a few years to work.

(I had never really been *persuaded* by Modernism in prose and have never quite grasped what Post-Modernism *is*. It was Evelyn Waugh, I think, who said that James Joyce went mad to please the Americans; Hugh's comments on the Modern do not go quite this far but are similarly bracing.)

Clark's work offered me constructional and rhetorical ideas. These influences haven't worked themselves out in open or obvious ways but stories of mine like "The Teeth of My Father", "The Eastmill Reception Centre", and *Private Parts: A Memoir* probably grew in their own dark from the seed of Clark's "Extractions and Contractions". I doubt that he'd acknowledge paternity.

It's probably also true to say, though, that Clark's stories fell into earth turned over by Ray. And that the first-person voice that speaks in them owes much to Hugh. And much in them is also my own. And Waugh's. And Roger Longrigg's. And Richard Yates's. And also, perhaps, *Toytown*'s Larry the Lamb.

Influence does not work in obvious ways and it's probably impossible to trace unless one person has consciously copied another. But I think writers' minds tend to seize on technical and rhetorical goodies — which is to say the same as emotional possibilities — and carry them off to the dark cauldron where they cook with and are changed by the other ingredients of the ever-simmering stew.

At the beginning of this memoir I said that MST was united only in its desire for honoraria. As a bond, that never loosened. But now, looking back, I think that we were held together by much more. We *grew* together. I don't think MST would have worked as it did unless we were getting from the association something more important than money. Four of us, at least, were writers obsessed by the idea of excellence, crazy about craft. MST gave us an association where craft was recognized and didn't have to be discussed; we were at home with each other, at home in the way that perhaps the disfigured are or the lame, that exiles are in a hostile land.

In my own case, at least, there was a sense in which membership in MST was a way of helping to *define* myself; the company of other writers I respected helped to confirm that I was a writer indeed. We were all younger then, of course, and our hilarity and arrogance masked an uneasiness.

We're all probably too busy now, too differently obsessed to spend time regularly in such readings. It's also probably true that we don't need each other in quite the way we did then. We all remain friends, of course, close friends, but we're living in different places, writing different things. MST was an almost accidental coming together which worked and grew stronger because we were who we were at that particular point in our lives. For three of us, at least, MST coincided, I think, with our apprenticeship.

Though we'd never have admitted it.

I had not thought much about MST in recent years before I started to write these recollections, but now I seem to see us as we were then and seem to hear those voices as we are driving down an endless road towards a reading somewhere — perhaps in the Maritimes.

We are all rather excited.

Ray Smith is being happily grumpy about the quality of food we can expect. Once when I was going out West I asked him if he had any restaurant recommendations.

"One cannot expect to eat well in Canada," he said, "*west of Guy Street.*"

What is he going on about now?

Lobsters. The wonder of lobsters from Cape Breton. The particular wonder of lobsters from his beloved Mabou. The impossibility of obtaining fresh lobster in New Brunswick. All lobsters are frozen and then exported to Toronto and then imported to Fredericton. Ray states this as fact.

Hugh offers statistics which prove that all foodstuffs in New Brunswick are 5¼% higher in price than in any other province. This leads on to arcane knowledge about distribution systems, capital, and monopoly. This, in turn, could well prompt Hugh to a discourse on the geography of distribution systems in the Canadian past, river systems, the Canadian Shield, glaciers . . .

But lobsters have prompted Ray Fraser to think of salmon which leads him into an amusing tale of poaching on the Mirimichi, a tale that involves guides, American tourists, and dynamite.

Smoked salmon.

I offer an observation about the only pizza place in Fredericton when I lived there. It not only dotted turd-like mounds of hamburger on the pizzas but it also proudly claimed: Made With Genuine Canadian Cheddar.

Clark is our resident French expert. So is Hugh but we're never sure if Hugh is making it up or not.

Ray Smith starts some French linguistic hare.

"What's the French for 'sanitary napkin', Clark?"

" 'Le Tampax'," says Clark.

" 'Cordon sanitaire'," says Hugh.

"Speaking of which", I say to Ray Smith, "remember that veal we had?"

"What veal?"

"In that restaurant in Old Montreal? Private house sort of place? Where the waiter said the can was upstairs and I went into a room where there was a woman watching television?"

"*I* wasn't with you. You must have been drunk."

"Sure you were!"

"No, I wasn't!"

"All right!" says Hugh. "Which one's this?"

As I sat in the bath-tub, soaping a meditative foot and singing, if I remember correctly, Pale Hands I Loved Beside the Shalimar . . .

"But *why* can't I have one of your fruit pastilles, Hugh?"

"Buy your own fucking fruit pastilles."

Slowing through a small town, Hugh winds down the window to shout gratuitous advice to a hairy youth.

Clark wants to know if we're going to be paid that night or later. He starts to explain how he has to cover some cheques for school fees or mass dentistry or tax arrears and this leads to discussion with Hugh — high financial stuff concerning mortgage payments and the portability of university pensions — discussion which does not grip the rest of us as we're variously unemployed or on the pogey.

Ray and Ray are debating in which order when they arrive they're going to drink:

Moosehead
Schooner
Tenpenny
Oland's
etc. etc.

Which prompts me to recall how after drinking Moosehead immoderately I was banned for life from the River Room of the Lord Beaverbrook Hotel in Fredericton for unplugging two amplified Spanish singers from St. John's.

Hugh starts to invent unlikely and obscene names for Canadian wines.

The voices play on and on.

The headlights unroll the dark.

On either side of the road, trees.

We are driving towards an audience.

Reading with Alden Nowlan at UNB, 1972.

Alden Nowlan, UNB 1972. In the background, Molly Bobak.

Group photo of Montreal Story Tellers by Sam Tata. Front: Metcalf, Fraser. Back: Smith, Blaise, Hood.

Montreal Story Tellers, 1975. Hood, Metcalf, Blaise.

Montreal Story Tellers, 1975. Metcalf, Hood.

Montreal Story Tellers, 1975. Hood.

Ray Smith.

Clark Blaise.

Montreal Story Tellers, 1975. Hood, Metcalf, Blaise.

Montreal Story Tellers, 1975. Hood answering questions.

Montreal Story Tellers, 1975. Metcalf, Hood.

A "Canada Day" in Montreal, 1975. Newlove at bay.

A "Canada Day" in Montreal, 1975. Metcalf, Hood, Doug Jones, John Newlove.

Photo by Sam Tata which was used as the cover of *The Teeth of My Father*. With daughter Elizabeth.

Reading with Alice Munro at Concordia University, 1975. Alice at right of first row. Clark Blaise seated far right.

Signing books for Hans Jewinski after a reading at Harbourfront in Toronto with Leon Rooke to celebrate the 10th anniversary of *Canadian Fiction Magazine*.

Metcalf, Rooke, 1982.

Hood, Rooke, Metcalf, in Ottawa, 1982. The first performance of a new reading group—*ECW Roadshow*.

Punctuation as Score

MANY READERS, IF NOT MOST, seem to think of punctuation merely as the utilitarian mortar between the blocks. They appreciate the stolid function of the full stop or question mark but when I start to talk of taking pleasure in the more delicate deployment of punctuation, eyes dull like morsels under old aspic. At professorial gatherings where the quicksilver banter is of tenure and mortgage, my recherché enthusiasms seem to be considered the mark of the dandy — or worse. After these brutal encounters, I am left feeling like the Ronald Firbank of Sassoon's account (*Seigfried's Journey, 1916-1920*).

"Anxious to entertain him appropriately, I bought a monumental bunch of grapes, and a glutinous chocolate cake. Powdered, ninetyish, and insuperably shy, he sat with eyes averted from me and my well-meaning repast. His most rational response to my attempts at drawing him out about literature and art was 'I adore italics, don't you?' His cup of tea remained untasted, and he quailed when I drew his attention to my large and cosy pile of crumpets. As a gesture of politeness he slowly absorbed a single grape."

In the following notes, I want to suggest that a preoccupation with punctuation is not exclusive to the wildly avant-garde or to the wiltingly effete but is a concern common to all writers who are alive to the possible music of prose.

Punctuation both for the fiction and non-fiction writer is primarily punctuation for the eye; the eye translates the symbols into stops and emphases. Yet at the same time, the fiction writer must also write for the ear; he must contend with the problem of dialogue. For many writers of fiction there is a conflict between ear and eye; the conventional symbols do not translate fully all the nuances of the voices that speak on the page.

(As a *further* complication, the fiction writer often has to *suggest* voice even when writing something other than dialogue or monologue. It is sometimes necessary to write in a modified third person which suggests an accent, an age, an occupation, etc. etc. and punctuation is an integral part of that suggested voice. The differences in voices are, in essence, differences in rhythm; punctuation helps in suggesting and emphasizing those rhythms.)

Standardization of punctuation started early in the nineteenth century and most of this work was carried on by the printers and compositors. Almost as soon as an orthodoxy established itself, fiction writers began to rebel against the tyranny of 'House Rules'. Dickens was one of the first rebels; his is an interesting and extreme example of the conflict between eye and ear. His experiments with punctuation were not so much concerned with dialogue as wholesale with the punctuation of the narrating voice.

The punctuation of *Oliver Twist* when it was first published in serial form (1838-41) conformed to 'House Rules' but by the 1846 book-edition Dickens had worked out a strange system of punctuation which operated as a musical score rather than as an aid to the understanding of syntax; in other words, Dickens had 'scored' his book for recitation.

The following quotation is from the *Standard Oxford Illustrated Dickens*.

> He had scarcely washed himself, and made everything tidy, by emptying the basin out of the window, agreeably to the Jew's directions, when the Dodger returned: accompanied by a very sprightly young friend, whom Oliver had seen smoking on the previous night, and who was now formally introduced to him as Charley Bates.

Even this punctuation is somewhat peculiar to the modern eye and would probably not have found favour with Partridge or Fowler.

The 1846 book-edition ran as follows:

> He had scarcely washed himself: and made everything tidy, by emptying the basin out of the window, agreeably to the Jew's directions: when the Dodger returned; accompanied by a very sprightly young friend, whom Oliver had seen smoking on the previous night; and who was now formally introduced to him as Charley Bates.

(This quotation is taken from the restored text of *Oliver Twist* edited by Kathleen Tillotson. The Clarendon Dickens. General Editors: John Butt and Kathleen Tillotson. O.U.P. 1966.)

The colons and semi-colons in this passage are extreme and irrational stops and suggest that the writing is intended for the boards and the limelights. The punctuation is irritating to the eye but less so to the ear; it demands to be read aloud — and read melodramatically. I find this punctuation almost impossible (as did many of Dickens' contemporary critics) because I don't want to sit in my armchair and declaim.

But whatever the obvious difficulties in departing from convention that this passage suggests, the idea of punctuation as 'score' has remained a central concern of many fiction writers. There have been varied experiments in this century which have added useful punctuational devices to the writer's technical stock; works by Joyce, Faulkner, Virginia Woolf, Dorothy Richardson, and e. e. cummings are obvious examples. Yet the experimentation of these writers was so extreme, so much a part of their individual voices, that their experimentation died with them.

No one in his right mind would consider my work 'experimental' but I've been trying for some years now to establish a system of punctuation which is more sensitive to voice than the conventions allow and which, at the same time, is not peculiar to my own individual voice.

I've failed.

And perhaps that's a good thing.

When Byron once criticized Leigh Hunt's style, Hunt said that his style was 'a system'.

"When a man talks of system," Byron said to Moore, "his case is hopeless."

However, an account of my failure might be interesting to readers to illustrate some of the technical preoccupations of writers of fiction. In what follows, I want to examine my use of quotation marks, italic, ellipsis, and paragraphing as ways of conveying *levels of voice*, as 'score'.

The rules for the use of quotation marks are simple. Words spoken are enclosed; words reported are not. Words spoken within spoken words are further enclosed by single or double quotation marks. Most publishing houses use double quotation marks for speech and single quotations marks within them for further speech. If the house uses single initial marks, then further speech is enclosed within double quotation marks.

Italic, where speech is concerned, is generally allowed only as emphasis or for such specialized purposes as indicating foreign words.

(It has been commonly accepted — and reasonably so — that italic should be used sparingly because if a sentence is correctly crafted the desired stress will be produced by the sentence's rhythm. This stricture applies, of course, more to expositional prose than to dialogue. The pepper pot sprinkling of italic has been seen by Men of Letters as a feminine characteristic — 'feminine' meaning, of course, semi-literate and breathlessly *girlish*.)

And with these rules thus stated, most authorities are content to rest.

Consider the opening of my story "Gentle as Flowers Make the Stones".

Fists, teeth clenched, Jim Haine stood naked and shivering staring at the lighted rectangle. He must have slept through the first knocks, the calling. Even the buzzing of the doorbell had made them nervous; he'd had to wad it up with paper days before. The pounding and shouting continued. The male was beginning to dart through the trails between the *Aponogeton crispus* and the blades of the *Echinodorus martii*.

Above the pounding, words: 'pass-key', 'furniture', 'bailiffs'.

Lackey!

Lickspittle!

The female was losing colour rapidly. She'd shaken off the feeding fry and was diving and pancaking through the weed-trails.

Hour after hour he had watched the two fish cleaning one of the blades of a Sword plant, watched their ritual procession, watched the female dotting the pearly eggs in rows up the length of the leaf, the milt-shedding male following; slow, solemn, seeming to move without motion, like carved galleons or bright painted rocking horses.

The first eggs had turned grey, broken down to flocculent slime; the second hatch, despite copper sulphate and the addition of peat extracts, had simply died.

"I know you're in there, Mr. Haine!"

A renewed burst of door-knob rattling.

He had watched the parents fanning the eggs; watched them stand guard. Nightly, during the hatch, he had watched the parents transport the jelly blobs to new hiding places, watched them spitting the blobs onto the underside of leaves to hang glued and wriggling. He had watched the fry become free-swimming, discover the flat sides of their parents, wriggle and feed there from the mucous secretions.

"Tomorrow . . . hands of our lawyers!"

The shouting and vibration stopped too late.

The frenzied Discus had turned on the fry, snapping, engulfing, beaking through their brood.

The use of single quotation marks round 'pass-key', 'furniture', and 'bailiffs' where double quotation marks would be considered correct has various effects. First, although they are words spoken *to* Jim Haine, they are not spoken to him directly face to face; a locked door stands between the characters. The "incorrect" use of single quotation marks suggests this distance. Second, Haine's attention is directed elsewhere and these three words are words his mind picks out from what is presumably a tirade. The words 'picks out' in the preceding sentence are important; were the three words in double quotation marks, they would be given greater weight and prominence on the page and this would weaken the intended effect of lack of attention to the harangue. The question of weight (or sheer blackness on the page, if you will) perhaps verges on calligraphy which is related to my third point. Single marks have the appearance on the page of pincers — as if the heard words have been 'picked out' from a flood of other words with tweezers.

The italicized words *Lackey!* and *Lickspittle!* while certainly fulfilling the allowable function of emphasis also do more. Because they lack quotation marks, they are to be understood as words not spoken aloud. But they *are* spoken inside Jim Haine's head to the man beyond the door. Italic hereby becomes interior speech — words formulated but not uttered. This device is now commonly used and commonly understood and has been for years yet it is not described or acknowledged in any of the standard reference works on punctuation.

With the words in conventional double quotation marks ("I know you're in there, Mr. Haine!") we are not only hearing the words of the man outside the door but we're also being made aware that Haine is hearing them too, that his agonized attention is being drawn from the tank of fish; he realizes that the noise has gone on too long and that the frantic parents will devour the fry. The double marks here contribute to action and to our awareness of Haine's consciousness.

Such a simple combined use of single and double marks, then, helps to establish the consciousness of the character and adds intensity and *drama* to his immobility and concentration. It also does away with the necessity of saying that he is rapt or staring fixedly or with great concentration. It also does away with having to say that the voice beyond the door was only half-heard or was muffled etc. etc. These effects could not have been achieved so economically and delicately had the conventions been observed.

(It is extremely important to note before going further that the use of single or double marks and italic in ways which differ from the conventional is only effective *because the convention exists and is expected.* The effect is much the same [or should be] as a denial of the ear's expectation in the established rhythm of a poem. The poet's departure from the established rhythm is usually to emphasize a key word or phrase.)

Quotation marks, single or double, have other functions which are widely understood but rarely, if ever, mentioned in books on punctuation such as those by Hart, Fowler, Carey, and Partridge. Most newspaper readers would understand the import of such a sentence as:

The Prime Minister stayed at the Lodge with his "niece".

Most Canadian and American restaurants, however, seem ignorant of the dangers of advertising their "famous" this or "delicious" that.

Quotation marks, then, also serve the purpose of irony or the negation of statement.

When I use quotation marks for ironic purposes, I prefer to

use single marks for what I suppose I must call calligraphic reasons — the single mark has a lighter, pincer-like, tighter-lipped, more *cruel* look than does the double mark.

The following is a quotation from "Girl in Gingham" where the experiences of a divorced man, Peter, are being recounted:

> Subsequently, with a large weariness and a settled habit of sadness, he had become active in the world of those whose world was broken. First it was the single women of his married friends' acquaintance, awkward dinners where he had learned the meaning of 'intelligent', 'interesting', 'creative', and 'kind'.

Single marks here are appropriate to tone and character; I would go so far as to say that they are an aspect of characterization. The irony implied in the single marks would have been too crude had the marks been double; the reader would have been bludgeoned rather than tapped or flicked. And as what I'm writing here is really *modified* third-person (i.e., something suggestive of Peter's voice rather than an omniscient voice) double marks would have been "out of character".

Peter goes upstairs after dinner to kiss his friends' little daughter goodnight and there then occurs the following which is a bridge into a passage of exposition:

> As Peter went upstairs, Alan in the kitchen was demanding his apron with the rabbits on it; Nancy's voice; and then he heard the sounds of laughter.
> 'The woman situation'.
> Whom, he wondered, had Alan in mind for him?
> The woman situation had started again for him some eight months or so after his wife had left him. The woman situation had started at the same time he'd stopped seeing Dr. Trevore, when he'd realized that he was boring himself; when he'd realized that his erstwhile wife, his son, and he, had been reduced to characters in a soap opera which was broadcast every two weeks from Trevore's sound-proofed studio.
> And which character was he?
> He was the man whom ladies helped in laundromats. He

was the man who dined on frozen pies. Whose sink was full of dishes. He was the man in the raincoat who wept in late-night bars.

The words in single marks in this extract — 'The woman situation' — are a repetition of his friend's question during dinner:
"By the way, nothing new with the woman situation, is there?"
Peter, then, is repeating mentally words spoken earlier. The words could have gone into double quotation marks or into italics.

If I had used double marks, the words would not have been differentiated from *spoken* speech. Double marks in no way suggest mental recall. Double marks would also have recalled more immediately the preceding scene where the words had been spoken when what I need is to move away from that scene and into a situation *interior with Peter*.

The single marks 'echo' Alan's question without repeating it *as speech* and so help to make a more natural bridge or transition into the succeeding passage of exposition.

The exposition begins at the paragraph: The woman situation had started again for him. . . . The writing here is in the third person but is carefully modified in its repetitions and rhetoric to suggest Peter's speaking voice even though he isn't speaking.

The movement towards the suggested inside of Peter's head is modulated in the following way:

1) The sounds Peter hears from the kitchen which grow fainter.

2) The words in single marks 'The woman situation' which recall speech but are not speech.

3) The words 'he wondered' in the next line.

4) The exposition of his past which is performed by the narrating voice taking on the colour and accents of Peter's voice.

This mental movement from exterior to interior is parallelled by his actual physical movements.

Peter is going upstairs. His progress up the stairs and away from his friends is marked by semi-colons. Also by Alan's actual heard *words*, Nancy's *voice*, then *sounds*. The external world retreats by means of semi-colons and the decline from *words* to *sounds*, leaving him alone and in silence.

The words 'The woman situation' could also have gone into italic but in this particular situation italic would have seemed too abrupt, too emphatic, too far removed from speech; to have used italic would have been an emphatic announcement almost as vulgar as saying:

"I am now bridging into a passage of exposition".

(The line in this extract — Whom, he wondered, had Alan in mind for him? — starts an interesting hare.

The handling of these He wondered ... He thought ... constructions has exercised writers for years. Convention demands that the words appear:

He thought, "She is the most beautiful girl I've ever seen."

The use of quotation marks in this kind of construction is monstrously unnatural because of the contradiction between *thought* and the implied *said* of the quotation marks.

I have seen writers try the following ways out of this particular horror:

1) He thought, 'She is ...
2) He thought: "She is ...
3) He thought: She is ...
4) He thought, she is ...

The colon here is far too heavy a stop and contradicts the essential *speed* of thought.

The most graceful solution I've seen was in a Philip Roth story printed in *The New Yorker* although I'm not sure if it's Roth's invention, *New Yorker* stylesheet, or simply growing American practice.

The construction was:

He thought, She is ...

This seems to me a delicate and triumphant solution to the problem and I adopted it the moment I saw it.)

It's always been my aim to make my dialogue as sharp and vibrant as possible by cutting out the use of explanatory adverbs and adverbial phrases — the irritating 'stage directions'. Getting rid of the adverbial mush makes heavier demands on the reader but dialogue should be crisp as a raw carrot and I can't pretend to feel interested in readers equipped with dentures.

Voices whose intonation and intent the reader immediately grasps offer writing a double benefit. The writing moves faster and is more vital but it's also true that the removal of adverbs creates the illusion of the invisibility of the author. The presence of 'stage directions' sets up artificiality within a single line.

"No, I will not!" he said, in angry tone.

Such a line as this offers us the voice of the fictional character but the 'realness' of this imagined voice is immediately countered by the intrusive 'authorial' voice telling us how to hear.

How much better to write:

"No, I will *not!*"

And let italic, the exclamation mark, and the reader's intelligence take up the strain.

In the following extract from "Girl in Gingham", Peter and Alan are about to complete an application form for a computer-dating agency:

> "Wait," said Peter. "How's all this nonsense supposed to *work?*"
>
> "You answer all these questions and then it matches you with someone who's given the same kind of answers. And then you end up with a Computer Compatible."
>
> "A 'Computer Compatible'?"

The final line probably fails to capture the voice I want the reader to hear because the single marks are being asked to perform a double function. The single interior marks are used more or less conventionally because Peter repeats Alan's spoken words. At the same time, I wanted the single marks to convey ironic comment in the way I use them in other places. I wanted the single marks to suggest Peter's scorn and unwillingness to cooperate. They enable us to do away with the tedium of:

"A Computer Compatible?" said Peter scornfully, in scorn, with distaste, uncooperatively, etc. etc.

It's more than possible that the circuits are overloaded here.
Pity.

The use of italics for other than conventional purposes has never, to my knowledge, been explored in Handbooks and Style Manuals. Apart from its use to indicate words thought but not uttered, it can suggest an amazing variety of voice and circumstance.

Consider the following extract from "Girl in Gingham" where Peter's experiences with a slightly potty psychiatrist are recounted:

> In the centre of Trevore's desk sat a large, misshapen thing. The rim was squashed in four places indicating that it was probably an ashtray. On its side, Trevore's name was spelled out in spastic white slip. Peter had imagined it a grateful gift from the therapy ward of a loony bin.
>
> It presided over their conversations.
>
> *How about exercise? Are you exercising?*
>
> *No, not much.*
>
> *How about squash?*
>
> *I don't know how to play.*
>
> *I play myself. Squash. I play on Mondays, Wednesdays, and Fridays. In the evenings.*

The words in italics are direct speech and should, according to the rules, go into double quotation marks. I chose to put them into italic for two reasons. First, they are part of a recounting of Peter's *past* experience in a purely narrative setting which otherwise lacks dialogue and to have introduced direct speech at this point would have disrupted the flow of a section of exposition precisely because spoken words (in quotation marks) would have jumped off the page assuming an importance they don't warrant. In contradiction to all authorities, italic here is *less* emphatic than words in quotation marks. Second, the use of italic here suggests the ritual quality of the conversation and somehow reinforces its silliness and sterility.

(A digression. For some years now, I've been playing with ways of producing economical caricatures of minor characters. Dr. Trevore rather pleases me. I like the way he is identified with the ashtray, the way he *is* the ashtray. I also like the rhythms of his italicized speech, the *oddness* of the rhythms. Dialogue is the fastest and most deadly way to describe a person. I'd go so far as to say that patterns of speech suggest even physical appearance.)

The following quotation from a shockingly bad story I once

wrote called "Playground" uses italic in a similar way but for slightly different reasons. A divorced father has gone to pick up his child at her grandmother's apartment.

As he'd gone into that familiar apartment building a feeling of bitterness almost physical had seemed to tighten his throat, a bitterness like the aftermath of vomit. He'd been surprised again at her grandmother's casualness, a casual amiability which seemed to ignore or even to have forgotten the recent past, the courts of law, the perjury, the pain.

The same scatterbrained flow of statements and the questions which did not wait for answers.

Are you still teaching those kind of people? Granny's bought her new pyjamas. 100% cotton. They're from Hong Kong so wash them before you put them on her. Everything from Hong Kong has Asian germs on it, doesn't it, my little angel? You've lost weight. Hasn't Daddy lost weight? Always buy cotton. So cute in her pretty dress that Granny bought her.

Goodbye.

The suitcase.

Goodbye.

And echoing after them along the corridor,

Buy her Spencer steak. It's the only kind she likes. Just like Granny buys her.

The reason for italics here is, I think, fairly obvious. The grandmother's words are not dignified with quotation marks because her words are sub-speech. Italics suggest better than quotation marks *prattle*. The use of italic, then, again becomes an aspect of characterization.

It seems to be a fact that unbroken italic is intensely uncomfortable to read. The expanse of italic here worried me and I felt compelled to break it up in some way. This led to a new invention — the dispensing with quotation marks around the non-italic Goodbye's.

Goodbye.

The suitcase.

Goodbye.

I was rather pleased with this effect because, calligraphically, it's so *flat* after the italic. And the calligraphic flatness parallels the emotional flatness and hostility. By their very flatness and lack of expected punctuation the words are undifferentiated from the object, the suitcase containing the child's clothes.

(All of this seems to me interesting and technically involving yet I must confess that at the same time this *particular* passage worries me. I'm interested in anything that can help in extending and amplifying the words on the page yet I'm also aware that experimentation with typography can degenerate into eccentricity and preciousness. Take e. e. cummings. Why the lower case name? What's the *logic*? Sometimes I think his "in Just- / spring" poem is genuinely fresh and that his typographic inventions indeed extend meaning. At other times, I think the poem is pukingly *cute*.

Any departure from convention is treading the high wire.)

The next quotation is from "Private Parts: A Memoir". It suggests another level of voice, a physical level, which italic can command:

The pervert's ritual was unchanging. He would trudge down the path wheeling his bicycle until he was about a hundred yards above us. Then he would prop his bicycle up on its little stand, turn his back, then turn again, mount, and peddle furiously down the steep hill. Just before he was level with us, he would swerve from the track onto the grass at high speed, coming to within five yards of us. By this time he was steering with one hand on the handlebars. In his other hand he gripped his member which he attempted to wave.

Then he would veer back onto the path and wobble down the hill to crash through the bushes at the bottom and debouch onto Gladstone Avenue.

His progress was unsteady and hazardous, rather like the charge of an inept knight whose visor has suddenly obscured vision.

When he neared us, we'd shout,

"Let's have a look at it, then!" and "My sister's is bigger than that!"

And as he careered away from us almost out of control down the bumpy hill, he'd yell, "You bastards!" and then, faintly, *Rotten bastards*, and then the crash as he engaged the bushes.

The words *Rotten bastards*, though spoken and heard, appear in italic here to suggest faintness of sound and distance and to hint at desperate pathos. Again, I think they lack the emphasis that italic is supposed to convey and had I used the "correct" double quotation marks, the effect would have been less funny — and less touching. There's something infinitely pathetic about the idea of a *failed* pervert.

The idea of using italic in this way doubtless came from that marvellous cry in comics as characters fall to their deaths from a great height:

AAaaaaa!

If we continue thinking of punctuation less as a formal series of stops and more as any devices which help to amplify and clarify the voice and its intent, then it's probably necessary for me to make a few remarks about paragraphing.

In general, paragraphing a line focuses attention on it powerfully.

Paragraphing of non-dialogue within dialogue is particularly useful in *orchestrating* dialogue — in building rhythms, in delaying the beat, in establishing pause and silence, and, by absence, in increasing tempo. Lines of non-dialogue within dialogue, if paragraphed, are not merely pauses and rests in the building of a rhythmic statement but suffer a change into something very close to dialogue itself.

The following passage from *Going Down Slow* is a fairly obvious example:

David sat down at his desk and while the kids found the right place in the book stared at the framed coloured photographs of the Queen and the Duke of Edinburgh.

"Peter, let's make up for lost time. 'Thou bleeding piece of earth'. Let's start there."

"I forgot my book in my locker, sir."

"Mary?"

"He's bleeding where they stabbed him."

"Yes, but 'earth'? Umm?"

Norvicki's face disappearing behind a large pink bubble which he deflated and engulfed again.

"Yes, Marjorie?"

"He's lying in such a lot of blood it looks like the earth is bleeding."

David shook his head.

"Support the Work of the Red Cross," said a poster at the back of the room.

"Yes, Ronnie?"

"Why couldn't he say what he meant, sir? I mean, if he's so good how come you can't understand him?"

The lines of non-dialogue here retard the pace of the dialogue. The scene is being dragged out because it is seen through the eyes of the teacher, David, for whom the class is an exercise in disappointment and dreariness. Dreariness and futility are the points of the dialogue; the interruptions of the dialogue intensify these feelings. The use of the present participle in 'disappearing' modifies the third-person voice making the perception closer to David and seemed to me to give the line the quality of answer to the preceding question; the expanding pink bubble becomes answer, becomes *speech*.

The following rather rude passage is from the same novel:

David mounted the stand and stood in the middle of the three stalls. He unzipped his trousers. Rubber footsteps squelched in the cloakroom. The swing-door banged open and Hubnichuk came in. They nodded. Hubnichuk was wearing a shabby blue track-suit.

He mounted the stand to David's left. Standing back, he pulled down the elastic front of his trousers. He cradled his organ in the palm of his hand; it was like a three-pound eye-roast. Suddenly, he emitted a tight, high-pitched fart, a sound surprising in so large a man.

Footsteps.

Mr. Weinbaum came in.

"So this is where the nobs hang out!" he said.

"Some of them STICK OUT from time to time!" said Hubnichuk.

Their voices echoed.

Mr. Weinbaum mounted the stand and stood in front of the stall to David's right.

"If you shake it more than twice," he said, "you're playing with it."

Water from the copper nozzle rilled down the porcelain.

There was a silence.

David studied the manufacturer's ornate cartouche.

The Victory and Sanitation Porcelain Company.

Inside the curlicued scroll, a wreathed allegorical figure. Victory?

Sanitation?

Mr. Weinbaum shifted, sighed.

"I got the best battery in Canada for $18.00," he said.

Again, the lines of what *seem* to be merely simple description are, in fact, mute dialogue. The ritual washroom remarks of the men, the rilling water, the words on the porcelain — all are *the same thing*, comments and statements. The passage also captures, of course, something of the studious silence of a shared washroom.

If I were writing this scene now — some ten years later — I would delete the phrase 'There was a silence'. It's not merely redundant; it is obtrusive. It's interesting to read this passage paragraphed conventionally.

Mr. Weinbaum mounted the stand and stood in front of the stall to David's right.

"If you shake it more than twice," he said, "you're playing with it."

Water from the copper nozzle rilled down the porcelain. There was a silence. David studied the manufacturer's ornate cartouche.

The Victory and Sanitation Porcelain Company. Inside the curlicued scroll, a wreathed allegorical figure. Victory? Sanitation? Mr. Weinbaum shifted, sighed.

"I got the best battery in Canada for $18.00," he said.

Here, then, is a totally different piece of writing, different in rhythm and different *in meaning*.

(One of the reasons why paragraphed lines of non-dialogue within dialogue approximate speech is purely technical. We are responding to convention. Convention decrees that each new speaker starts his speech on a separate line as a new paragraph. Because we are trained to respond to that convention, we are unconsciously half-prepared to read the lines of non-dialogue as being closely related to direct speech.)

I've so far deliberately chosen examples which are extreme the better to illustrate the idea; the following example from "Girl in Gingham" is more subtle, perhaps, and certainly more typical. The situation is that Peter has gone to the house of a woman he's never met whose name has been supplied by the Computer Dating Agency. The conversation is awkward and nervous.

"Well," she said, "you must tell me all about appraising. What does an antique appraiser *do*?"

"Well," said Peter, "furniture's the bread-and-butter side of . ."

"That's a dip I make myself," she said, lifting a white limp leather handbag from the floor by the end of the couch and rummaging.

"'But porcelain and silver," said Peter, "are my . ."

"And I'm sorry about the chips — I was rushed and picked up those awful ones that taste of vinegar by mistake — but the dip's very good. It's very easy in a blender — sour cream and Danish Blue, chives, and a teaspoon of lemon juice."

She found cigarettes at the bottom of the bag.

"Delicious," said Peter. "Absolutely delicious."

And listened to himself crunching.

"Tell me," she said, snapping and snapping the mechanism of the slim lighter, "we didn't seem to talk about this, did we? Or did we? I was rather flustered — well, *you* know, and my memory's awful but did you say you *weren't* married? My memory! Sometimes I can't even seem . ."

"No," said Peter, leaning across and lighting her cigarette with a match. "No, I'm not."

"You're lucky," she said.

He smiled and then sipped.

"Peter," she said, "you listen to me. You pay attention. You're a very lucky man."

Paragraphed lines like, And listened to himself crunching, are intended to work on various levels simultaneously. In that Peter is listening to himself, it implies that the awkward conversation has come to a stop, that there is an equally awkward silence. Peter listens *to himself* — emphasizing his lack of involvement with the woman. 'Crunching' is in itself vaguely funny but with its suggestions of breaking and destroying also painful. The line serves to end, and summarize, a cycle or fit of the conversation. It seems to me that the line almost becomes a comment on the whole situation *by Peter*. While remaining, of course, in the third person.

The following lines from the same extract suggest another way in which speech can be punctuated:

"Tell me," she said, snapping and snapping the mechanism of the slim gold lighter, "we didn't seem to talk about this, did we? Or did we? I was rather flustered — well, *you* know, and my memory's awful but did you say you *weren't* married? My memory! Sometimes I can't even seem . ."

"No," said Peter, leaning across and lighting her cigarette with a match. "No, I'm not."

The words which interrupt speech — snapping and snapping the mechanism of the slim gold lighter — serve various functions. First, they halt her question and create, in the smallest way, tension and suspense. Second, they *parallel* her difficulty in asking the question. Third, the word 'snapping' functions in much the same way as did 'crunching' referred to earlier.

Peter's reply and described action *cut across* her babble both verbally and physically, the described action paralleling the words. Peter's "No", because it is separated from the rest of what he says ("No, I'm not." which *softens* that first "No") takes on somehow larger significance than an answer to the question. It is a "No" to the whole situation.

I've sometimes listened to actors in CBC studios who have been recording readings of my stories and on various occasions they've wanted to dispense with 'he said' or 'she said', instinctively wishing, perhaps, to turn story dialogue into stage dialogue. The placement of such simple things as a 'he said' or 'she said' can be of vital importance. What *profound* differences there are between:

"What do you think you're doing?"

and

"What," he said, "do you think you're doing?"

Prose has its own necessities.

Much of what I've said so far is too intuitive and personal, relies too heavily on context, to be of *systematic* use to other writers. Systems cannot be expounded when one is constantly forced into using words like "seems", "suggests", and "calligraphy". But there are two unconventional devices I use — minor fragments of the Grand Design — which *could* be used systematically by other writers because neither device depends on context or the writer's sensibility.

The first of these devices is particularly useful in crowd scenes.

Imagine two people talking at a party. The writer wants the words of others to impinge on their central conversation. Such "overheard" conversation might be vital for later plot development, colour, contrast, comedy, or for "fragmented exposition". Yet at the same time, the writer wants the dialogue to remain crisp and uncluttered by such irritating stage directions as:

A voice behind me — The fat man to his left —

Convention requires us to use double quotation marks for all speakers. In what follows, A and B represent the "foreground" speakers and C represents the voice "overheard" by A and B.

A: "So what did he do about it?"
B: "Well, by this time, of course, he was crazy with rage
and he . . ."
C: "I know what you mean. I've always felt uneasy about
George's appetites."

The words spoken by C *might* have been spoken by A again in
response to B. I've deliberately chosen words for C which might
be interpreted in this way to illustrate the problem by exaggera-
tion. Two pages like this and most readers would be hopelessly
confused and irritated. Stage directions are necessary.

A: "So what did he do about it?"
B: "Well, by this time, of course, he was crazy with rage
and he . . ."
C: "I know what you mean," said the man beside the
potted palm. "I've always felt uneasy about George's
appetites."

At first glance, there seem to be no great problems with such a
construction as this but imagine the annoyance of such identifications as 'the man beside the potted palm' repeated over two
pages.

Again, the conversation between A and B, the foreground
speakers, might be an intense and passionate conversation.
Frequent visual identifications (the man beside the potted palm)
might suggest that A and B are constantly looking about them
when what the writer wishes to convey is that they are locked
visually together. Stage directions force the authorial voice to
become obtrusive; the reader is aware of manipulation.

A writer of great power and elegance, Keith Waterhouse,
uses what I feel to be a very clumsy device for handling this
problem. In the following extract from *Jubb*, two men in a pub
have picked up three girls. The five are joined by a third man.
The third man (A) is the first speaker. The words in brackets
and quotation marks, a mechanically indignant question, are
from (C) — one of the girls in the background of the conversation.

A: "No, really," I said, "I must go now."

B: "You're not leaving us to handle three of 'em, are you?"

C: ("Do you mind?")

A: "I'm afraid so."

What is so *very* wrong with Waterhouse's invention is that the weight of the brackets and double marks drags what should be in the background to the foreground.

I was delighted, however, to discover that we were both bothered by the same problem.

My solution is simple and, I think, elegant.

And can be stage-managed over pages if necessary.

Retain double marks for A and B and use single marks for C. A mixing of double and single marks enhances such a scene by suggesting physical distance and lower volume for the words in single marks.

The second device I use in dialogue which might be used by others is the awful ellipsis.

The standard use of the ellipsis in dialogue is to indicate omission.

As in:

"I'd like to have a word with you if you . . ."

Here we understand the uncompleted completion of the sentence to be something like "if you can spare the time" or "if you don't mind". Reading the line and seeing the ellipsis the eye gives the signal to the voice to fall or waffle or "shuffle" forward slightly to suggest continuation.

The ellipsis instructs the voice to extend 'you'.

(Depending on context, the ellipsis can suggest confusion, embarrassment, vagueness — all manner of things.)

What our conventional system of punctuation seems to lack is a mark or stop which indicates the *interruption* of one speaker by another. Some writers use a dash but a dash has other uses — one of which is to indicate a *pause* — and is therefore possibly confusing.

My invention, if it *is* an invention, is to use a two-point ellipsis instead of a three to indicate interruption. Some such device is important because it scores for the reader the *pacing* of the exchange.

It looks like this:

A: "I haven't the slightest idea," she said, "where they . ."
B: "Why? Why haven't you?"
A: "Well, it's all rather . . ."

A's first line is to be read as if the conclusion of the sentence is coming. In other words, there's a fast breath-check on 'they'. A's second line is to be read with a conventional 'waffling' on the word 'rather'.

Another use of this two-point ellipsis is to indicate the *continuation* of a sentence after an interruption. Imagine three speakers.

Thus:

A: "I've always been very fond of . ."
B: "So shall we buy it or not?"
A: ". . a nice ham sandwich. I always say that you can't beat . ."
C: "Who'll give us a loan?"
A: ". . fresh bread and a nice slice of ham."

I think this device is genuinely useful and fills a need. Most of the time I find myself using it for comic purposes.

I wonder why?

My failure to erect a system doesn't really trouble me. I have too much humour in my make-up to join the ranks of Spelling Reformers or Universal Esperanto Speakers. But it would be a mistake, I think, to dismiss these notes as merely eccentric or obsessionally technical. The reader must remember that punctuation is a means to an end. There is nothing odd or silly about the desire to transcribe or create voices in such a way that the reader can immediately grasp their full range and intent.

Voices speaking are the heart of literature.

Punctuation helps us hear.

Without an 'E'

MY FIRST STINT as a writer-in-residence was at the University of New Brunswick. I was offered the appointment through the good offices of Kent Thompson, a fellow writer and a professor in the UNB English Department, who argued that the university should assist younger writers instead of automatically piling honours on those already laden.

I had first met Kent when he was editor of *The Fiddlehead*, the literary magazine which has been associated with UNB for so many years and which has done so much to encourage young poets and fiction writers. In 1970, Kent organized under the umbrella of *The Fiddlehead* a conference of writers and critics to discuss the current state of fiction in Canada. It was Kent's conviction that the critics were years behind the writers and he hoped the conference might stimulate some of them to grapple with the sudden sophistication that Canadian fiction was exhibiting. Nothing of the sort happened, of course, but it was interesting and instructive to meet, among others, Hugh Hood, Dave Godfrey, Rudy Wiebe, and David Helwig.

Dave Godfrey was then a bright star in the firmament of Canadian Letters having helped found The House of Anansi and having written a bulky and ultimately incomprehensible book called *The New Ancestors*. He now teaches Creative Writing. He was at the time rabid with nationalism and my accent and antecedents seemed to rub him up very much the wrong way; at breakfast in the Lord Beaverbrook Hotel he read the stock market reports in a marked manner. I was relieved to discover, however, that his rage was general; during a perfectly unexceptionable paper by Professor Hallvard Dahlie entitled "Self-Conscious Nationalism in the Novels of Hugh MacLennan", Godfrey suggested that Professor Dahlie would benefit from "a good bum-fuck" administered by Scott Symons. This was a form of ideological re-education which had not previously occurred to me.

My appointment as writer-in-residence at UNB grew out of

this conference and out of fiction I had been publishing in *The Fiddlehead* and coincided with the collapse of my first marriage. During the academic year 1972-73, I was largely *non compos* through grief and drink but Fredericton is a better place than most in which to go mad because one's foibles there are less remarkable. A couple of years ago I was chatting to Kent about old times and made some comment about the general *looniness* of Fredericton; he corrected me sharply pointing out that during the time I was there the loony one had been me.

I haven't the nerve to argue the point *strenuously* but . . .

Soon after my arrival, I was summoned to the office of Desmond Pacey, the University's Acting President. The interview was brief and rather like a small boy's introduction to the Headmaster of the boarding school. It went something like this:

"I have read your novel *Going Down Slow* and consider you at least the equal of Mordecai Richler."

"Thank you very much but I don't really . . ."

"And perhaps better in that your satire is more sharply focussed."

"Well, I . . . er . . ."

"I am myself a writer and I'd like to" — opens desk drawer — "present you with this inscribed copy of *The Picnic and Other Stories.*"

The stories were unfortunate but I must say that Desmond Pacey was the only example of Top Brass at any university I've been associated with who ever thought it important enough to say hello — let alone to have read any of my work. It's well worth remembering that he championed Canadian literature at a time when such enthusiasms were even less respectable than now.

Duly inducted, I sat in my office wondering what would happen next. I was supposed to make myself available to students who wished to talk to me about their writing. Other than that, the time was my own to get on with my own work. This was, of course, impossible.

I am unable to write unless the omens for the day are propitious. My paper must be of the correct shade of yellow, the ink black, the pencils 2B. The wind has to be sitting in the right quarter, the barometric pressure such and such. There must stretch before me uninterrupted time free of anxieties. Even the knowledge that three days ahead lies an appointment with the dentist is enough to render the idea of work ludicrous.

Such neuroses control my activities at the best of times. During this particular year I was busy getting divorced twice from the same woman and was crazed with worry about my small daughter who was in the legal care of my wife and therefore exposed to my wife's lover, a peculiarly irresponsible lesbian photographer who wore boots and suspenders. There seemed little point in setting pen to paper anyway, even if I'd been able, because the moment I'd got a phrase down, students would have appeared with manuscripts.

I sat listening for human sounds.

My office was between those of poets Robert Gibbs and Fred Cogswell. Robert Gibbs often held long discussions in his office with students about Pre- and Post- Confederation poets none of whom I'd read. He also had briefer and more interesting chats with his bookcase, briefcase, and filing cabinet.

Fred Cogswell used his office as warehouse and editorial centre for *Fiddlehead Poetry Books* — an enterprise distinct from *The Fiddlehead*. He was always extremely affable and kept me abreast of the doings of all his poetesses. These conversations were baffling because his starting point was always an outcropping of some hidden lode.

An entirely typical exchange would run as follows:

"She's feeling a lot better now."

"Oh, hello, Fred. Pardon?"

"Much closer to a decision."

"Oh. Good."

"We went for a long walk on the beach on Sunday."

"I see."

Silent puffing on his pipe.

"His big mistake, you see, was to offer marriage."

"Mistake?"

"It offended her deeply."

"Oh."

I had no idea to whom these daily bulletins referred and so they all combined in my mind into a composite, into an Identikit Portrait of a *Fiddlehead Poetry Books* poetess — youngish, good-looking, sexually unhappy or inverted, offended at elemental levels by the world's *coarseness*, terribly sincere, terribly sensitive, terribly intense — in sum, not unlike the Madeleine Basset to whom Bertie Wooster often refers.

The students with their wads of manuscript did not arrive.

During that entire year at UNB, I saw two students. When I was writer-in-residence at the University of Ottawa, one student came to see me; she was in the English Department and wanted to know if I thought she should quit. She seemed very intelligent so I advised her to quit forthwith. We still correspond. When I was writer-in-residence at Loyola of Montreal not a single student appeared. When I was writer-in-residence at Concordia one student did come to see me but he turned out to be an unpublished poet seeking my aid in securing a teaching position at a CEGEP.

At four universities, then, at great cost to the universities themselves and to the Canada Council, I had dealings with three students. At these four universities I was asked only once to address a class. And honesty compels me to admit that the professor who *did* ask was one given to the bottle who regarded teaching as a chore disruptive of serious drinking.

I suspect I lack mass appeal.

But if I was not exactly overwhelmed by the flattery of student attention in Fredericton, I did enjoy friendships with some of the faculty. Most of the members of the English Department were extremely pleasant and affable — an unusual state of affairs as I discovered in subsequent appointments. The only member of the English Department who seemed less than jovial was its head, Professor David Galloway, who described me and all other Canadian writers-in-residence as "travelling mountebanks". But shortly after my arrival he returned to England to supervise the publication of Elizabethan voters lists or some damn thing, taking with him, it was rumoured, some $500,000 of Canada Council funds.

The University of New Brunswick has a well-deserved reputation for its support of the arts; it maintains painters and musicians as well as writers. Alden Nowlan is something of an institution in New Brunswick and it is greatly to the university's credit that they have helped to support him through years of illness and financial uncertainty.

Alden's house on the edge of the campus has become a mecca for visiting writers and for hosts of young poets who drop in for encouragement and the ever-present gin. Evenings with Alden always begin with great affability but the emotional direction of the evening can veer as the level in the gin bottle drops. Or on some evenings, bottles.

Alden is a very large man. Operations on his throat for cancer have left his voice growly and this, combined with his bulk and beardedness, suggest a huge bear as he sits in his armchair rumbling and roaring about the monarchy (he supports the Stuart Pretender) or about the paucity of scientific evidence for the world's being round (he's a founding member of the Canadian Flat Earth Society).

Alden was brought up in a small village in rural Nova Scotia in conditions of dire poverty. He is, proudly, self-educated. But he is also prickly on the subject and is likely to attack and bait visitors for the relative ease and comfort of their circumstances demanding to know how with their obvious gentility they can hope to understand "life".

To hear Alden's account, he never saw paper or pencil until the age of twenty-five. Some professorial visitors seemed to feel shame at their lack of humble origins and at their ordinary fathers who hadn't eaten the bark of trees to sustain life etc. etc. Alden derived a great deal of entertainment from these exercises.

When I once suggested that fifty-two ounces of undiluted gin was going at it rather hard, he countered by saying that where *he* came from he was not accounted a drinker.

I was rather bored by the romanticism of the idea that the life of New Brunswick peasants was somehow more "real" than the life of, say, Toronto stock-brokers and I used to tell him to stop talking balls. It was at about this point that the evenings degenerated into rumbling abuse.

But inside the big growly frame there's a teddy-bear. Alden is basically good-natured and sentimental and remarkably tolerant of younger poets — if anything, too tolerant and kind in that he'd rather encourage the desire than judge the performance. And if he is on occasion bullying and abusive — it's usually the gin talking.

I was always rather surprised that someone of Alden's background and struggles in life was not automatically of the political left. I never really did discover where he stood politically but I suspect that his interest in and love of ritual, display, hierarchy, and past splendours suggest an emotional stance somewhere far to the right, not an unusual ground for poets.

I've always admired his early poetry, the poems in *The Rose and the Puritan, Under the Ice, Wind in a Rocky Country*, but with his *Bread, Wine, and Salt* — which won the Governor-General's Award — an aspect of his temperament which I consider detrimental to his poetry began to receive intensified expression. Some of the poetry became far too prosy and he gave in to the desire to be warm, wise, and "philosophical" — cracker-barrel philosophy. At the end of that road lies the *Reader's Digest*.

The arguments that Alden and I had on sentimentality were ferocious.

Early poems like "Palamino Stallion" show great subtlety, chastity, and delicate control and so it's particularly surprising that Alden's short stories are, in the main, rather lumpy. The voice that in the poems is colloquial becomes in the stories folksy. The collection *Miracle at Indian River* is somehow journalistic, a part of a North American tradition from which I feel particularly estranged. They are 'tales', for the most part, rather than stories and I distrust the honesty of the teller. I believe the voice in the poem "Cousins" but I don't believe the voice in "Miracle at Indian River".

Robert Gibbs handles the same sort of material with far greater skill and sensitivity in his story collection *I've Always Felt Sorry for Decimals* — a book dedicated to Alden.

(One of the great pleasures of Fredericton is to hear Bob Gibbs reading these "artless" stories which he claims, with typical modesty, were written to entertain fellow faculty members. A line from his story "Get on Board, Sinners" by the young child, Pompman, who is on a train journey through the New Brunswick bush and sees a barn deserves immortality in a book of Canadian quotations:

"Look," said Pompman, "there's some civilization again.")

The early seventies were exciting years for Canadian literature. Literary presses were being established, literary magazines sprouted like wild flowers, the American Ogre was being prodded with bold sticks. For a few years there even seemed to be the beginning of an audience. Now, this literary revival is over. What audience there was has melted away. And having got rid of *Time Magazine*, we're lumbered with *Maclean's* — every bloody week.

Three graduate students in the English Department at UNB were part of that early ferment; while completing their degrees, John Moss, Dave Arnason, and Robert Sorfleet were plotting the first issue of the *Journal of Canadian Fiction*. Some of my own work appeared in the first issue and for subsequent issues I did interviews for them with Clark Blaise, Alice Munro, and Mordecai Richler.

(Richler, by the way, seems to be getting bad press recently and photographs have tended to show him propping up bars and looking hunted. I'd like to record that he is gentle, kind, and dignified. If he's been snarling of late, it's doubtless because reporters ask him stupid and offensive questions. If it is indeed *true* that he asked on a TV programme who Anne Murray *was*, then he deserves a medal.)

The *Journal of Canadian Fiction* was, from the very beginning, a magazine divided against itself. It was an uneasy mixture of fiction and criticism. The criticism often illuminated corners of the Canadian literary attic which should have remained dusty and undisturbed. Criticism of more recent work tended to be thematic, of course, and therefore of interest only to teachers and sociologists. The editors were by inclination and training academic and the fiction they published was, in the main, dreadful. This was because most of the fiction submitted to them was dreadful but it was also because the editors were young and simply had not read enough outside the confines of Canadian writing to have developed an informed taste. The *Journal* somehow never developed a *personality* and its format and design were unpleasing and amateurish. The magazine lingers on to this day but rarely publishes engaging writing.

The history of the *Journal* is a paradigm of the renaissance, "flowering", and death of Canadian literature.

The driving force behind the *Journal* was John Moss who is personally a most pleasant and engaging man but whose writing reveals a mind more than somewhat confused. The thesis he was completing while I was at UNB became the book *Patterns of Isolation in English Canadian Fiction*. I read some small part of the thesis in draft form and offered some suggestions about vocabulary and syntax. But obviously too politely. That Moss's second book of criticism *Sex and Violence in the Canadian Novel: The Ancestral Present* could have passed scrutiny by outside readers and by the editorial machinery of *McClelland and Stewart — The Canadian Publishers* and *still* conclude with the breezy line, "This ... is the view from one corner of the circle" suggests why excellence in Canada is rarer than unicorns.

(Moss's most recent critical work, *A Reader's Guide to the Canadian Novel*, is, if possible, even worse. His ludicrous praise of my novel *General Ludd* is an embarrassment and his comparing me as a comic writer with Cervantes, Fielding, Trollope, and "Waugh at his very best" should be grounds for dismissal from any responsible university.)

The year in Fredericton ground on for me.

I played darts a lot. I helped to found the Writers' Union of Canada. I chaired a committee made up of Margaret Laurence, Alice Munro, Fred Bodsworth, and Timothy Findley which was responsible for drawing up the criteria for membership. There was a deep split from the very beginning between those who wanted a union and those who wanted something close to the idea of an Academy. Everyone, however, feared that the proposed union might become merely another Canadian Authors Association and any accommodation seemed worth avoiding that fate; the chasm between those who were frankly elitist and those who were unionist was papered over. We compromised eventually by making membership dependent on having published a trade book (i.e., a non-textbook) with a non-vanity press. Acceptance or rejection of an application for membership, however, lay with the Membership Committee.

I served on the National Executive of the Union for three years but quit in umbrage over Graeme Gibson's proposal that the Union supervise the putting together of a series of anthologies for school use. I had nothing against missionary work but I argued that if this were done the contents of the anthologies would seem to have Union *imprimatur*; that it would seem as if the Union were saying 'This is Canadian literature'. My other strong objection was that the anthologies were thematic in structure. Producing a book called, say, *The Immigrant Experience*, reduced the stories and poems in it to mere illustrations of sociology and history. In other words, I felt that the thematic approach to literature was anti-literary.

(I needn't have worried, of course. The books did appear. They had as much impact on our school systems as tossing pebbles into a big swamp.)

I loved the euphoria of the first meetings, the sense of community, but the union grew larger and its ranks filled with people who had published genuine trade books but *what* books: Cook books, bizarre Litcrit, kiddy books, how-to books etc. etc. The union soon bulged with people I'd never heard of and didn't want to know. Pierre Berton even held forth on the desirability of closed-shop politics. I *should* have felt a sense of solidarity in that all were writers of books but I didn't, and don't.

There was a strong sense of fantasy at all times for me about the union in that we were all practitioners of a craft on its way to extinction trying to sell our wares to an audience which had forsaken books years earlier for TV in a nation where the federal government admits that close to a quarter of the population is functionally illiterate. It was all rather like shrill field mice delivering very stern warnings indeed to rows of unblinking owls.

There is something uneasily comic about the idea of court action by a union which is subsidized by the government against a publishing company which is also subsidized by the government; one wonders to what the string above one's head is connected.

Whenever I moan to my wife about the writer's plight, she says I should consider myself lucky they don't come for me in the middle of the night.

Totally missing the point, of course. The writer in Canada can write *anything*. Nobody reads it. And certainly not 'they' who can't even burn down a barn efficiently.

I do sometimes miss the union but I was one of those who from the beginning had hankered after an Academy — deep leather chairs, a pension from a grateful State, and Old Scrotum, the wrinkled retainer, tottering forth with the brandy and soda.

When the end of the academic year arrived, I returned to Montreal unemployed and broke. I was not sad to be leaving Fredericton although I'd made good friends there. I'd found the atmosphere of the town claustrophobic and I looked forward to eating in some good restaurants again. Or, given the state of my finances, eating pizza again which was not manufactured with cheddar cheese and dotted with dogmounds of hamburger.

In the years since I've left, I often find myself thinking about a particular evening I spent with Molly and Bruno Bobak. I tend to wonder about it while shaving or as I'm drifting into sleep. Bruno was most generous with his excellent home-made wine, each bottle bearing a label of his own design. When I awoke next morning and investigated the world, I discovered that the entire right knee of my trousers was missing. It seemed to have been *burned* out. I examined my flesh for signs of conflagration but it was unblemished.

It remains one of life's unsettling mysteries.

In Montreal I was lucky enough to pick up a part-time teaching job at Loyola. Loyola was, for me, a kind of home. The relationship in the past had been stormy. I had been one of thirteen who had gone on strike against the college for its abrupt and unreasonable firing of a scientist from India. We were fired, in turn, by telegram. The strike spread. The college was placed under CAUT censure. The campus filled with under-employed RCMP constables, easily identified because they were healthy-looking and pressed joints on all and sundry. The Montreal *Gazette* even went so far as to allege that the thirteen of us were funded from Peking. Why the Chinese communists would wish to fund thirteen rather disreputable layabouts was not made clear. We were all eventually re-instated through the legal intervention, free of charge, of Brian Mulroney.

My days during the strike had been spent with fellow lecturer Sean Kelly, who later became an editor of the *National Lampoon*, writing and inventing scurrility directed against the unyielding Jesuit hierarchy. My only regret about the whole vastly entertaining episode is that an utterly wicked piece I wrote for the student newspaper — a piece involving the college's president, Father Malone, in unseemly doings — mysteriously disappeared from the newspaper's offices. Perhaps this literary gem will turn up one day when my RCMP file is open for inspection.

Looking back now with the advantage of years of hindsight, I realize that my enjoyment of a good fight betrayed me; I was on the wrong side.

Somehow I got through the summer, even managing to do some writing, and when the next academic year began, I found myself sharing an office with Loyola's new writer-in-residence, Al Purdy.

I have never done much teaching while I've been a writer-in-residence but I have taught Creative Writing in colleges and CEGEPs largely because I'm only possessed of a B.A. and the educators consider me unfitted to deal with more weighty matters. In the last CEGEP in which I worked, Vanier College in Montreal, I was even disbarred from teaching a course on the Canadian short story because I lacked the necessary qualifications.

I'm often asked if I think Creative Writing *can* be taught. Or *should* be taught. I'm probably the wrong person to ask in that I believe *contemporary* writing shouldn't be taught. Contemporary writing is what one reads for pleasure. It is too close to us to judge and evaluate. At university one should study the classics.

But perhaps I'm just thinking of a distant dream.

The sad truth is, I suppose, that if contemporary literature were not propped up by the universities, we'd have much less of it than we do.

'Creative Writing'.

I've always liked the joke about the brain-surgeon at a dinner party who says to a writer:

"When I retire, *I'm* going to take up writing."

Replies the writer,

"What an *amazing* coincidence: When I retire, I'm going to take up brain-surgery."

Creative Writing is always listed on Evening Courses along with Fondue Cooking, Macramé for Beginners, Creative Flower Arranging etc. etc. One does not see Brain Surgery listed on Evening Courses. There is the mass delusion abroad that writing is something anyone can do with a little effort.

Brain surgeons are not resented by the populace. The populace has brains enough at least for *that*. But we live in such an egalitarian age that if the writer says, 'My poem or story takes as much skill and talent, and perhaps more, than does brain surgery', he is dismissed as an elitist swine of the first water. Indeed, the idea of *good, better, best* is one with which a goodly part of the populace is unhappy. Everything, well, simply *is*. If the reader doubts this, let him engage a class of high school students.

It's salutary to remember that not long ago surgeons, in slack periods, busied themselves doing hair-cuts and shaves.

Many university students of creative writing simply can't accept that something they've expended time on is less than perfect. Their attitudes often remind me of the Monty Python skit about the Pope informing Michaelangelo that he is not satisfied with *The Last Supper*.

"You *don't* like it?" says Michaelangelo in disbelief. "It took me *hours*."

The students we have now are presumably the result of years of child-centred education where the infant, tot, child, and stripling was endlessly and lavishly praised for every creative splotch and blot. They come to me interested in *expressing* themselves. They are all very sincere. They have read *nothing*. And, even more interesting, have no *intention* of reading anything. They lack humility. And, odds on, couldn't spell it. They wish, simply, to write. The worst write most.

If praise is not forthcoming, they tend to say things like, "Well, that's only *your* opinion". This *can* lead into hours of mindless twaddle on the subjectivity of aesthetic response but I learned years ago to say, "Yes, it *is* my opinion and my opinion is more informed and therefore more valuable than yours. Which is why I'm sitting *here* and you're sitting *there*". This can result, with luck, in the student's quitting the class in high dudgeon.

I am, of course, talking about *graduate* students.

Most write badly in vaguely traditional modes. Some, far worse, have jumped from the Hardy Boys to James Joyce and write in a *very* peculiar stream of consciousness. I have had only one or two students in years of teaching who were capable of dismantling a story by, say, Katherine Mansfield, and explaining how it works. And that, of course, has little to do with *writing*. Though it's an essential preliminary.

When I read Amis' *Jake's Thing* I immediately recognized the female undergraduate who said she thought Hamlet was a woman. When pressed for reasons, she said she didn't *have* any particular reasons, she just thought he was.

To talk to most of these students about *style* is to incur their deepest suspicion and hostility.

The whole dreary experience reminds me of Waugh's review of Stephen Spender's autobiography:

". . . to see him fumbling with our rich and delicate language is to experience all the horror of seeing a Sèvres vase in the hands of a chimpanzee".

If the reader thinks all of the foregoing is merely undiluted bile, he should ask himself: How many students of creative writing in Canada go on to publish their work in the literary magazines? How many of *them* go on to publish a first book of stories or a novel? How many of *them* go on to publish a second book?

Enough said.

But even if I have had bad luck in the students who have come my way, there are still powerful reasons for feeling less than happy about the idea of teaching creative writing. The relationship between teacher and student is always coloured by emotions but in creative writing the emotional component is at the centre of the relationship.

The student invests in a short story or a poem far more personal emotion than he does in an essay on, say, the activities of the Wheat Board. The student *identifies* with what he has written; any criticism of the story or poem is taken as a criticism of its author. This is perfectly understandable; such feelings afflict writers who have been publishing for years. If the teacher criticizes the logic of a paragraph or points out that dialogue sounds stiff and unnatural, it is a rare student who can accept and understand the criticism. It is *normal*, given the context, for the student to be defensive; he is defending *himself*.

If the student gives in to the obvious authority of the teacher, he must give up a part of himself; he must allow himself to be dominated. Domination is always accompanied by resentment. Indeed, the resentment may be so great that no real learning has taken place. Yet, if the student resists instruction, that is, clings to and defends *himself*, no learning takes place either.

The whole 'creative writing' exchange, however politely and lovingly carried on, seems to me, unavoidably, an exercise in authority and subservience — and therefore doomed. All teaching implies subservience to authority but subservience to the rules of punctuation or the multiplication tables is not the same sort of subservience which is implicit in the relationship between professional writer and neophyte. Nor is the relationship the same as that between master and apprentice. Between those two stands a physical product — a chair, a gold ring, a mosaic — some visible example and standard of physical perfection towards which the apprentice can strive.

The apprentice is not likely to sulk if his first mortise and tenon joint is not snug. Its lack of perfection is obvious even to the apprentice. The authority in the relationship between master and apprentice resides less in the master than in the perfect artifact. It is unarguable. The apprentice writer *should*, similarly, bend the knee to the classics, to the tradition, but appreciation of literary greatness is, to an extent, subjective. Even the basics of literary style are not as immediately graspable as the basics of cabinet-making. The great literature of the past does not offer an *obvious* blueprint for the apprentice. A short story or poem is not a mortise and tenon joint and its lack of perfection is *not* obvious to the beginning writer. Blinded by love which is, in effect, self-love, the student simply cannot see the flaws which are so obvious to his teacher.

Creative Writing digs other pitfalls.

There is a temptation for the teacher however much he fights against it to teach *himself*, to suggest solutions to problems which are the solutions *he* has arrived at over a long career, to favour the styles and shapes which approximate his own. Some teachers are even attracted to and flattered by the idea of disciples.

Some students *and* teachers engage in Creative Writing because of the intimacy of workshops; they thrive on heightened emotions. Students who are unconsciously in search of fathers or lovers and teachers who are motivated by — I hope unconscious — lusts, persuade themselves that they are gaining and giving insights into Art when they are actually being titillated by scarcely sublimated sexuality.

(Alice Munro once said to me that she thought weekend and residential 'workshops' were so popular because they produced a climate conducive to fornication.)

Most students simply do not understand that affecting art is produced by the austere manipulation of technique. If they did understand this, most would feel repelled. Most students are *nice.* Not very bright — but nice. Most seem to think that writing has something to do with sincerity.

I have grave reservations, then, about creative writing, because of the nature of the emotional relationship between teacher and student. But for all my reservations, I am faced with the fact that Iowa *does* turn out writers. And some very good ones. I'm not sure what the secret is but I expect that they accept as students only those who are already publishing and who are already capable of distancing themselves to some degree from their work. And, with the school's reputation, they draw the best from all over the U.S.A. and Canada.

But even Iowa cannot teach the central and unteachable mystery of style.

When I look back on the early part of my own career, I *think* I can see the way *I* learned. My first stories were atrocious. Had someone pointed out to me their obvious defects I would have felt angry and would have defended the stories to my last breath. To this day, I can't be objective about my own work until it's cooled off for some months, until I'm no longer much connected with it. When I say "cooled off", I don't mean to imply that my emotions are identical to the emotions aroused by the story but rather that at the time of writing I'm hot convinced that the technique of the story, the machinery for the delivery of *its* emotion, couldn't be bettered. After a period of time, I'm always disappointed. Which serves as a spur to try harder.

I began to learn about my own deficiencies when I could re-read work from the year before *and feel embarrassed.* The ability to feel embarrassed was the result of incessant reading of fine story writers with close attention to their technical manoeuvrings. Perhaps the best school of writing is reading — and writing itself and sending out the inadequate products to literary magazines and being rejected. These years out in the cold are an excellent education. I'm sure there are talented young writers who never get as far as a book because they're not prepared to pay the price. Being a professional writer of the literary persuasion requires substantial talent but it also requires endurance. During the last twelve years of Canada's literary renaissance, growth, decline, and fall, I've seen reputations rise like rockets and I've been deafened by the clatter of falling sticks. An important part of being a writer is digging in for the long siege and ordering your life in such a way that you're not countermined by alcohol, marriage, despair, or journalism.

Meanwhile, back at Loyola . . .

Al Purdy was not actually in residence. He commuted from Ameliasburg. This involved him in endless pre-dawn train rides during which he was forced to fortify himself against the bitter cold. By the time he arrived at the college in the early morning he was often fortified to the gills, cheerful but sleepy. He solved this problem by having a collapsible cot moved into our office and locking the door.

He surfaced at midday, phoning a nearby grocery store to deliver cases of beer to the office. He soon after that warmed the place up with a comfortable fug of cigar smoke. He used to fill in the boredom of the afternoons by scouring Montreal's used-book stores for Canadiana and first editions always returning with a few more volumes for what must be by now one of the largest private libraries in Canada. It is rumoured that he trades wads of Purdy manuscript for particularly choice volumes. Although he pretends not to be, Al is very sensitive and scholarly and his knowledge of editions and their points is extensive.

He is a man of strange contradictions perfectly illustrated by the following anecdote. I once visited him when he was writing-in-residence at some prairie establishment. I found him in a modern apartment block. The apartment was unfurnished. By that, I mean that except for broadloom on the floor and three cardboard cartons containing his possessions, the apartment possessed not even a chair. There were a few bottles standing about and some disgusting empty cans which had contained beans and Irish stew — presumably his meals over the preceding days. We sat on the floor drinking and chatting about who was where and who'd been publishing what. By his side was a box of books he'd just acquired from a local dealer. He began to gloat about them. He teased me for a while, knowing my interests, and then reverently drew out a first edition, fine in dust-wrapper, of Evelyn Waugh's *Scoop*.

Al's classes in creative writing were held in our office. There were five or six students in the class. I have no idea of what abstruse matters he pursued in these classes but whenever I passed by he seemed to be playing records of *Under Milk Wood*, of Richard Burton reading Thomas, and of Cyril Cusack's wonderful, breathy, fluttering of Gerard Manley Hopkins. I somehow gained the impression that, as a teacher, Al was not notably severe.

The academic year ground on.

With the advent of spring and the retreat of the snow under our office window, beer bottles began to surface, more and more every day as the sun gained strength, until they lay revealed on the playing field like corpses after a mighty battle.

The following academic year I was once again forced to find part-time work and ended up at Vanier College, Snowdon Campus. It was an unspeakable employment. The year was saved by the fact that I had one good student, now an actress in Toronto, and by my office being adjacent to that of Barry Cameron — now a professor at UNB — who was being driven insane even faster than I was. We sustained each other by mutual bemoaning as we picked our way through the, literally, ankle-deep litter in the corridors. Barry had led a fairly sheltered life in a university up until then and could scarcely believe what had signed up for his thoughtful courses in Canadian literature. He had no idea of how fortunate he really was; I used to describe other CEGEPs to him such as Darkest Dawson where whip and kitchen chair were standard issue for all tamers and where Eric Partridge could have recorded grammatical and syntactical uses of the word 'fuck' hitherto unknown to scholarship.

(e.g., *As a mode of address* — as a substitute for 'you' or for a person's given name as in; "Hey, fuck!")

Compared with this Black Hole, the Snowdon Campus of Vanier College was a haven. The word 'campus' is misleading; it suggests lawns and manicured flower-beds. The college was housed in what had been an office-block and fronted onto the Decarie Expressway. Immediately next door was a large A and W. With the windows closed, the heat was intolerable; with the windows open, it was impossible to make oneself heard over the traffic. The chairman of the English department had retired from the fray; he used to lock himself in his office with the Head of the Remedial Programme and gaze at a cassette of *Deep Throat*.

To make ends meet, I also taught an evening course at Loyola.

Loyola's replacement for Al Purdy was John Newlove.

John is a man of impressive skills; I remember being in his office once in Toronto when he was an editor at *McClelland and Stewart*; he was talking to me, talking on the phone, and correcting intricate copy all at the same time. But I've never been able to imagine him *teaching*. He often spoke of his desire to dismember various versifiers who plagued him at Loyola but I expect that face to face he was, as usual, courteous, diffident, and charming. It is only when under the influence that he bites. And by 'bites' I don't mean 'becomes snappish'; John *bites* people. Nobody knows why. At receptions in his honour, at convocations, after public readings, at literary parties, screams will suddenly cut through the chatter. He seems to bite friend and foe impartially. But it's a minor eccentricity for a major poet.

I have one memory of John and Susan that year that might stand for many others. We had been drinking and talking until dawn and it had been agreed that the next day, or rather, later in the same day, they would come and dig me out of my apartment and we would go to my favourite shop in Montreal, the Petit Musée on Sherbrooke Street, where I would introduce them to its owner, Max Klein, and where we would browse among pottery and antiquities.

The day dawned, for the second time, in the afternoon. John looked a bit ragged round the edges and I felt more than a little fragile. At the Petit Musée I performed introductions and then we wandered around lusting variously — Susan lusting after Ashanti goldweights, John after some small Greek pots, myself after a very rude Bayaka fetish that I'd had my eye on for some time.

John wished to examine a small ampulla or alabastron which was decorated with a band of dog-like creatures. This small pot was in a locked glass cabinet. Mr. Klein switched on the lights within the case and unlocked the door. The spaces between the glass shelves were narrow and the shelves themselves were crowded with fragile Egyptian, Greek, Etruscan, and Pre-Columbian pots and faience figurines. The alabastron-thing (I've always maintained that the 'dogs' are, in fact, Attic ferrets) was crowded in at the back of its shelf.

Mr. Klein is getting on in years and his hands have developed a slight tremor. Because of this, fearing that he might smash something, he asked John to reach in. But John was afflicted by morning-after shakes and was in a worse way than Mr. Klein. I offered to help but found that my hands, too, were atremble.

It was a weird and rather surrealistic sight to see inside a lighted glass display cabinet three twitching, shaking, trembling hands.

Susan was making anxious sounds behind us, doubtless convinced that the glory that was Greece was soon to be expensive shards.

One of the disembodied, dancing hands reached further in.

Susan, in an agony of apprehension, cried out a warning and somehow stepped sideways into a large red-lacquered Japanese drum sort of thing which fell and exploded into a surprising number of its component staves.

Of course, we cursed her roundly.

Mr. Klein, glumly polite, said that miracles were possible with epoxy.

Another memory of that year — for me, oddly uncomfortable and unsettling. I had taken John to a Writers' Union party held at Hélène Holden's house in Westmount. The unstated purpose of the party was to make overtures to the French Canadian literary establishment. Nothing much came of the venture — possibly because so few English Canadian writers present were able to speak French. Those French Canadian writers to whom I attempted to speak in my few words of Welsh-accented French immediately replied in flawless English. The pain was probably too much for them. Hubert Aquin was, as usual, the centre of attention; he was more soigné than usual and was being devastatingly charming.

John had had too much to drink and as the evening progressed drank even more and became openly belligerent; he was working himself up to avenge an imagined slight. I thought it prudent to engineer a departure before someone got the business-end of a bottle and so called a cab and somehow persuaded

John into it. In the cab, he was silent and angry except for a few cryptic mutterings. It was a silence which was to last for years.

> I am too tense,
> decline to dance
> verbally.

As we had left Hélène's house, I had looked back into the warmth of the living room. The people to whom Aquin was holding forth were roaring with laughter.

A year later, he shot himself on the grounds of the Villa Maria convent.

At some time during this Vanier year of suffering I was invited to the University of Ottawa to give a reading. I happened to bump into the chairman of the English Department, Professor Glenn Clever, who said quite casually,

"Oh, by the way, would you like to be writer-in-residence here next year?"

"Yes," I said, "thank you."

"Fine," he said. "I'll send you a contract," and pottered off.

It is difficult to find measured language with which to describe the English Department of the University of Ottawa as it was then and with which to describe my experience of being writer-in-residence.

I will begin with a few facts. It was agreed that I would make myself available to students (as it turned out, all one of them) two days a week. I was commuting from Montreal and sleeping over in Ottawa for one night. The Department had known months in advance of my arrival. When I duly presented myself at the English Department offices on the first day of term, I was introduced to the new chairman, Professor Marcotte. He informed me that my office was at the top of the old house which serves as English Department offices but that unfortunately the room didn't have a desk in it. Or chair. There was, apparently, something wrong with the heating system so that the temperature in the room was stuck at over 100 degrees.

I returned to the Lord Elgin Hotel.

It took three weeks for the desk to appear.

The chairs took another two.

Two weeks before I left, my arrival was announced.

Members of the English Department did not seem to speak to each other. I said hello to Seymour Mayne in the corridor but he hurried away. Everyone seemed strangely *guarded*. The air was thick with atmosphere. It was rather like dropping in to visit acquaintances who were in the thick of a peculiarly nasty marital battle.

I soon locked polite horns with Professor Marcotte who wrote triolets.

The year before, my name had been solicited by the University to appear on an advisory editorial board for the volumes of short stories being published by the University Press. I had agreed to this. I was never consulted about anything and never even advised of what they intended publishing. I urged upon them a couple of ventures — publishing a selection of Kent Thompson's stories and republishing Audrey Thomas' *Ten Green Bottles* but nothing came of my urgings. I arranged eventually for Audrey's collection to be published by *Oberon*. And then they announced a selection of Leo Simpson's stories. It didn't bother me at all when they were publishing the work of the long dead — republishing the stories of Isabella Valancy Crawford held for me about the same level of fascination as digging up old clay-pipe stems — but it annoyed me considerably when they intended publishing the work of the living — at a royalty of only 8%.

And Leo a union member, too.

When I arrived at the university, I remonstrated with Professor Marcotte. I pointed out to him that although there were some pretty ropey contracts in Canada his was undoubtedly a lulu.

Comically 'correct' correspondence started to pass between us.

Professor Marcotte claimed that his hands were tied, that all decisions were in the hands of an ancient Oblate in the recesses of the library.

I urged him to excavate this Oblate and stir him around a bit.

Professor Marcotte asked me if I were prepared to put at risk the entire publishing programme for the sake of a paltry 2%.

I assured him that nothing would give me greater pleasure.

Relations deteriorated to the point that I was forced to

threaten adverse publicity and 'blacklisting' by the Writers' Union.

I began to get the impression that Professor Marcotte thought that I was not a gentleman.

He was right. And I won.

Deskless, chairless, studentless, I was bored out of my mind. To while away the time I decided, pinching Kent Thompson's idea, to organize a conference on the short story — an extravaganza of writers and critics. There were public readings by an All-Star Cast which included Clark Blaise, Hugh Hood, Kent Thompson, Alice Munro, Ray Smith, Margaret Laurence, and Audrey Thomas. Critics included Bill New, George Bowering, Barry Cameron, Patricia Morley, Frank Davey, Doug Barbour, and Michael Dixon.

The whole affair was introduced by Robert Weaver of CBC *Anthology* and it pleased me immensely to be able to pay tribute, in however small a way, to Bob's immense contribution to Canadian writing and to his unfailing support of writers over so many years.

I often think of my first crazed weeks in Fredericton and of the phone ringing suddenly in the silence. Bob Weaver had somehow found out where I was and phoned to offer support and encouragement — and to commission a story because he knew I'd need money. I was paid in advance and immediately but he had to wait a very long time indeed before I was able to write again. People like Bob Weaver and Margaret Laurence — who comforted me in time of trial with generous sympathy and scotch — have not only helped and encouraged countless young writers but have handed on an ideal of kindness and service to the tradition of writing. Margaret describes writers as her 'tribe'. Some might consider that sentimental but I don't.

I had gathered together the necessary money for this conference from the Canada Council and from the U. of O. Student Council; the English Department confined its support to insisting that papers be signed indemnifying it in case of financial shortfall. At one point, enraged and sickened by the department's *pissy* attitude, I offered in writing to make good out of my own pocket any loss that might be incurred. As the complexities of the conference grew, the flow of "official" paper between Professor Marcotte downstairs and me upstairs must have amazed and confounded the secretary in the middle who had to type it all. She must have thought the whole business demented but, typical of the department, never said a word nor raised an eyebrow. The faculty members seemed incurious; they struck me less as a community of scholars than as a gathering of soured accountants.

I can't remember the university's official motto but if the attitude of Professor Marcotte was anything to go by it was probably: *Cover Your Ass.*

As the conference approached, my days were spent on the run booking hotel rooms, booking the Press Club, arranging for rooms and an auditorium in the university, checking sound systems, writing letters, phoning, confirming, soothing.

But in spite of the department's marked lack of enthusiasm and in spite of the fact that I was forced to apologize to all the guests for the niggardly hospitality and the department's legalistic insistence on its limited financial liability — no, George, I'm afraid that if you phone home from your hotel room to tell your wife and little ones that you arrived safely it must be understood that the University of Ottawa — despite all this contemptible and niggling parsimony the conference was a great success. The readings drew crowds of about three hundred students and the critical papers audiences of fifty or sixty.

The University of Ottawa had promised to publish the papers presented at the conference but of course reneged.

A couple of the critical papers were a disgrace. Of them I will say nothing. Some were negatively interesting. Frank Davey's paper on Clark Blaise was astonishing in that he seriously advanced the view that Blaise's writing was akin to journalism — this of one of the country's most *poetic* writers. My jaw dropped lower the further he got into the thing. Patricia Morley, seemingly blind to literary form and style, delivered, at great length, what was, essentially, a series of plot summaries of Margaret Laurence's African stories and drew some fanciful and wrongheaded conclusions. No surprises there. But George Bowering gave an involving and quirky paper on Audrey Thomas and Doug Barbour was entertaining and stimulating on Ray Smith's work. And despite the fact that there's no love lost between us, I'm forced to admit that Bill New's brief paper on Alice Munro was the best thing yet on her work.

The academic year ground on.

Correspondence with Professor Marcotte slowed to a trickle.

At the end of my six-month tenure, I gratefully made way for some other poor bugger.

On my return to Montreal, Elspeth Cameron offered me a job as writer-in-residence at Loyola for the balance of the academic year. I remember complaining to her that not a single student had wished to see me; she seemed surprised that I was perturbed since she'd assumed that I simply wanted to write. The idea of disinterested patronage made me uneasy; I was always waiting for the other shoe, as it were, to fall. I did very little at Loyola other than prop up the Faculty Club Bar with old friends, notably the brilliant and naughty Harry Hill who when he feels inclined teaches me about poetry.

At about this time, Hugh Hood had published *A New Athens* and my wife and I went for a drive with him one day to look at Athens and the surrounding countryside. We decided that it would be a pleasant area in which to live and were soon looking at houses. We were attracted by a stone farmhouse in Delta, a village about ten miles from Athens; that Delta was in the Township of Bastard clinched the matter as far as I was concerned. For the next five years what gold I earned was transmuted by reverse alchemy into concrete and two-by-four as our bargain mansion slowly revealed itself as a precarious ruin.

One afternoon in 1981 while I was watching the corn grow and wondering how I was going to get through another year with no visible means of support, Professor Henry Beissel phoned offering me a year as writer-in-residence at Concordia University.

During the previous two years in Delta I'd been writing *General Ludd*. I had worked on it every day for long hours and when it was finished I felt terminally exhausted. Before *General Ludd* I had written *Girl in Gingham*. I had also taken over editing *Best Canadian Stories*, first with Joan Harcourt, then with Clark Blaise, and then with Leon Rooke. I had also edited various text books and had edited some story collections for *Oberon Press*. I had launched a new series called *First Impressions* designed to help young writers reach a larger audience. I had contributed occasional essays and introductions to this and that, written reviews, and, regularly, judged grant applications for the

Canada Council. My wife and I had two children from previous marriages and had also somehow managed to acquire guardianship of two Chinese refugee teen-agers from Saigon and had adopted two small children from an orphanage in India.

I was tired.

My literary labours over the years had been rewarded, however, by an entry in the *Supplement to the Oxford Companion to Canadian History and Literature*.

I was, at last, world famous in Canada.

Actually, I was *uniquely* rewarded in that I won *two* entries in this compendium.

One entry was under METCALF, JOHN.

The other entry was under METCALFE, JOHN.

I was tired and I was also broke.

The offer by Henry Beissel of the Concordia job was providential as manna but the post meant more to me than money. I would be returning to the city where I had lived so long and where I had started my life in Canada; I would be returning to Montreal to a building right next door to the one where I'd stayed on my first night in Canada — the YMCA. But I was no longer a shy immigrant shocked by the brazen doings in the YMCA showers; I was no longer a high school teacher; I was no longer a struggling young writer ignored by lofty academics. I was returning as Visiting Dignitary, as Man of Letters.

These weekly trips to Montreal promised entertainment and diversion, restaurants a shade more rigorous than those in Brockville, the relaxing pleasures of old friends. They also offered an absence of children — in itself a positive good.

As the beginning of the new academic year approached, I made preparations.

I bought a new jacket.

My wife cut my hair.

On the train that was bearing me to Montreal I felt expansive.

I spotted *three* red-tailed hawks — a particularly good omen.

The first thing I saw in the corridor at Concordia was a poster advertising the public reading I was to give that night.

The poster said:

"Well-known novelist, short story writer, and editor, now appointed Writer in Residence at Concordia for 1980-81".

My name was prominent in heavy black capitals.

Messy, white, liquid paper disfigured the poster's pink ground.

It was doing a poor job of concealing the 'E'.

Editing the Best

DESPITE THE PLENTIFUL GREY HAIRS I see every morning in the mirror, it still came as a shock to me to realize that I am about to write something which can only be described as history.

I came to Canada in 1962 on a ship called the *Carinthia*. It was a miserable voyage; I started vomiting when the ship was still attached to the dock in Liverpool and continued well past Trois Rivières. As the *Carinthia* drew into the mouth of the St. Lawrence I was blind to the opening wonders of the New World. My world had contracted. Again.

Although I was entirely unaware of it then, 1962 was the year that Hugh Hood published with *The Ryerson Press* his first book, the story collection *Flying a Red Kite*. The *Carinthia* has long gone to the breaker's yard, *The Ryerson Press* survives only as a hyphenated appendage of *McGraw-Hill*, and Hugh Hood, now working on his eighteenth or nineteenth book, is no longer quite so fresh of face as the young man who is looking out of the window on that first dust-jacket.

I came to Canada more or less by accident. I could as easily have gone to Hong Kong or Australia or Burma. I applied for a job with the British Council in Lima, for a job as a manager of a plantation in Burma. I nearly secured a job in a private school in the West Indies but proved "unsuitable" after questioning the pittances to be paid to my various servants.

The great attraction of all these places, and of Canada, was that they were not England.

After leaving university, I had drifted into a job in a Secondary Modern Boys' School in Bristol. It was a school over-stocked with the sons of the proletariat and run by a man who was clinically insane. My flat was in the once-fashionable Georgian and Regency area of the city where I had lived as a student, huge limestone houses in rows and crescents divided now and subdivided into flats, flatlets, and bedsitters but still beautiful in their decline. The bus journey from my flat to the Bluebell Secondary Modern School was an expedition to another world.

The bus lumbered down towards the city centre, through all the commerce, on through the drab streets of terraced houses and small shops — newsagents, fish and chips, turf accountants — towards the decaying prefabs and the rawness of the housing estate served by Bluebell School. The invisible dividing line between the city I lived in and the city I worked in was marked for me each morning by a butcher's shop whose windows announced in whitewash capitals:

UDDER 9D PER POUND.

This daily journey soon presented itself to me as a metaphor. My life was split between a decaying past which exercised a great power over me and a present which was unbearable and stretched ahead like a life sentence. Even then, I realized that it was futile and deadening to live for the past and I knew that I had to get out of England and escape from its dream.

Had my job been interesting and comfortable, I'd doubtless have succumbed to the dream and lived out the rest of my life clad in tweed with vacations spent taking brass rubbings in medieval churches. But life at Bluebell Secondary Modern was neither interesting nor comfortable. The school was a compelling argument against the desirability of compulsory education. The staff were caricatures. The headmaster was downright alarming. The pupils ranged from the merely drooling to the psychopathically loutish.

It was the sort of school where homework was rarely assigned because the pupils returned with notes written on torn brown bags which said:

Dear Teacher,
He have not done his sums because its
bad for his nerves
Thanking You I Remain
Signed Mary Brown (*Mrs*)

The remedial mornings were divided by School Dinner from the remedial afternoons.

In a container of medieval proportions, greasy stew studded with emerald processed peas followed by steamed pudding and aluminum jugs of custard topped by a thickening skin.

When emissaries of the Protestant School Board of Greater

Montreal set themselves up in a suite in one of the city's posher hotels to drum up custom, I was one of the first in line.

The formalities were simple. I merely had to furnish evidence of sobriety and moral probity attested to by a Minister of Religion and the results of a Wasserman Test proving that I was not riddled with pox or clap. I promptly wrote a sickening letter and signed it as the Vicar of St. Michael and All Hallows and some days later took my place in a long line of subdued Jamaicans at the Bristol Royal Infirmary's v.d. Clinic. Two men in white lab coats were indulging themselves in unseemly badinage with the clientele.

When my turn came, one of the men said,

"Well then, where have *you* been sticking it?"

"I haven't recently," I said with some asperity, "been 'sticking it' anywhere. I'm not here for medical reasons. I only need a test because I'm emigrating."

He stared at me.

Then he shouted,

"Hey, George! Come over here! You're not going to believe this but I've actually heard a new one!"

The high school to which I was posted had a reputation, I was warned, for toughness. Rosemount High was in the eastern part of the city — the area that in those carefree days of Anglo power was referred to as "the French part". Compared with any British secondary modern school, this reputedly tough establishment was like a luxury rest-home.

After an initial period of gawking at the strangeness of everything and after figuring out, theoretically, the shape and extent of Canada, for, typically and criminally, I had been ordered to teach Canadian history, I began to look about me to find the literature.

What follows, then, is an impressionistic sketch of how Canadian literature appeared to an immigrant teacher of literature in the early sixties.

The first observation I made was that there was precious little literature in evidence. Nor did there seem to be much of a literary world. The literary landscape was dominated by Hugh MacLennan, Morley Callaghan, Hugh Garner, Sinclair Ross, and W. O. Mitchell.

(Margaret Laurence had at this time written little and

Richler's first books were published by Deutsch. Both were living in England.)

As far as the schools were concerned, awareness of Canadian writing was restricted to MacLennan's *Two Solitudes* in a bowdlerized version, the odd story by Callaghan, a handful of poems by Bliss Carman, Archibald Lampman, and Sir Charles G. D. Roberts, and one or two pieces by that Monarch of Mirth, Stephen Leacock. Everything else was British and American with the scales heavily weighted on the British side. And horrid stuff it was. Bad poems of the W. H. Davies variety and arch, personal essays of the "On Preparing To Garden" school. It was as if students and teachers had been caught in a time-warp which preserved the faded diction and gentilities of what had been a peculiarly barren and bankrupt period in the literature of the "Mother Country".

The literature was a perfect complement to the *social* environment which the school board was attempting to maintain — or imagine. This also was British — school uniform, divisions into 'Houses', discipline backed by violence, decorum. Teachers were imported every year from England to stiffen the system's backbone. It was a colonial situation analogous with, say, modern Nigeria.

In brief, it would not be unfair to say that in the early sixties in Canada the literature being taught and celebrated was some of the worst that had been produced in England in the first thirty years of this century.

Even the literary revolution of the seventies has not broken that strange loyalty to outmoded forms. The awful tradition of consciously "comic" writing which expired in *Punch* so many years ago has been institutionalized here with the Stephen Leacock Award for Humour which honours staggeringly unfunny books which are positively archaic in sensibility. It's interesting to compare a contemporary collection of Canadian humorous pieces with the work of contemporary practitioners in England such as Patrick Campbell and Paul Jennings. Or with much earlier practitioners in the States such as Thurber and Joseph Mitchell.

Or even Ring Lardner.

This "dead hand" of bankrupt tradition which seems to me so typical of Canadian literary history is exemplified by the

Canadian branch of P.E.N.   A world organization of writers dedicated to protesting against electrodes on genitals is, in Canada, an organization which is confined to Westmount. Everyone in Canada *not* in Westmount is referred to as an *out-of-town-member* — a marvellously myopic phrase. The Canadian branch of the organization does not vehemently concern itself with human rights; it saves its energies for tea and buns with favourite sons like Sir Edwin Leather.

In the early sixties, Montreal was far more sophisticated than any other city in Canada. Let us not speak of the other cities. Those students who were bright and desirous of being hip were plugged into a certain extra-curricular awareness of poetry by the precious buffooneries of Layton and Cohen who were showing the flag for literature in the city's bistros, taverns, and universities. The female population was peculiarly open to instruction.

It's a sad comment that such flag waving was necessary.

Cohen's poetry was exactly right for the 12–16-year-old "naughty" set. Romantic stuff, rebellious, not too difficult to grasp, touches of surrealism which were whimsical rather than arresting, and all produced by a handsome young man who "suffered" prominently. Why his poetry ever engaged adults always baffled me. His later dirges such as the world-famous "Suzanne" are, of course, pseudomystically incomprehensible which doubtless explains their popularity.

Layton was, and is, a considerable poet.

Prose, however, lacked any such charismatic practitioners.

Callaghan struck me as an extremely *clumsy* writer. I was not charmed by the obtrusive didacticism of the novels nor by their cardboard characters. The stories, which were accounted better than the novels, seemed to me even worse. They were badly written and mawkish. The language was plodding. I was offended all the time by Callaghan's telling me what every damn thing meant; he was unable to leave the reader alone.

Recently, one of the early stories, "The Little Business Man", was reprinted in the *Reader's Digest* and it's hard to think of a more fitting home.

Sinclair Ross is a much better writer but it's *As for Me and My House* which commands respect rather than the stories. John Moss has recently called the stories in *The Lamp at Noon* "some of the finest in the language". Most of the stories are basically plot stories; when we've found out "what happens", we've gone a long way towards exhausting them. The language and imagery are, however, much more involving than is usual in plot stories. They're *good* plot stories but finally they're only that. To say of them that they're "some of the finest in the language" is to invite comparison with Hemingway, Katherine Mansfield, James Joyce, Eudora Welty, Caroline Gordon, Flannery O'Connor, Thurber, Lardner, Anderson, Faulkner, etc. Which is to be foolish.

There is a considerable element of poetry in Ross's stories — particularly in the best stories such as "Cornet at Night". The weakness of the stories is that the insistence on "meaning" often clashes with the *experience* of the story. The stories are far too much *tales*; they are deformed by plot. Ross is unable to let meaning grow from our experience of the story's world; he editorializes. "Cornet at Night" is brutalized by Ross's final paragraph which summarizes and explains the story. In "One's a Heifer", as another example, there is some good and involving writing, particularly the rather complicated identification of the physically damaged owl with the mentally damaged farmer, but our experience of place and person is diluted by the demands of the form Ross chose to write in — the "whodunnit" or "whodunwhat"; story writers would not now choose a form which crippled their real interests. Ross is a writer who, in his stories, was poised for flight but remained earthbound, weighted down by traditional baggage he was unable to jettison.

(*The Lamp at Noon* in the New Canadian Library edition is introduced by Margaret Laurence who was influenced by Ross at quite a young age. She is a vastly more sophisticated story writer than Ross but it's interesting to note that she, too, in the stories in *A Bird in the House* often intrudes to summarize or add obtrusive comment. This is particularly noticeable in "The Loons" where the story is progressively weakened by the final two paragraphs. It is almost as if her trust in the reader falters. It is puzzling to compare this story with the very much earlier work in *The Tomorrow Tamer* which contains such glowing stories as "The Perfume Sea".)

Hugh Garner's writing is primitive and uncouth.

(I remember Garner writing a piece for me to accompany a

story in an anthology for students. I wrote back questioning a few points of grammar. He replied:

"Change whatever you want. Hell! It isn't Holy Writ".

Any writer who *doesn't* regard his work as Holy Writ is not worth much time or consideration.)

The only writers of stories who might have become interesting figures were Ethel Wilson and Raymond Knister.

In 1962, Hugh Hood published *Flying a Red Kite*. This was the first book of modern stories published in this country. Or perhaps it might be more accurate to say 'traditionally modern'. These stories were in the line of descent of all modern stories. Relatively few people have grasped how centrally important this book is to Canadian literature. The stories have withstood the passage of the years magnificently. The only bad story in the book — significantly enough a story first published in *Esquire* and quite uncharacteristic of Hood's genius — is "After the Sirens". For the rest, they are as fresh as the day they were first written.

So it had taken some forty years for a world movement to impinge on Canada. The interesting question is how Canada had managed to remain almost untouched for so long. The monuments of the modern movement were as available to Canadians as they were to anyone else; they were no further away than the nearest bookshop. It seems that Canada was isolated from the rest of the world by some inexplicable time-lag. Raymond Souster as late as the fifties and sixties, for example, was still working in what was basically an Imagist manner. A partial explanation may be a ponderous conservatism and the total lack of an informed audience. I haven't read enough to *know* but I have a suspicion that literature in Canada up until, say, 1950 was so largely crappy because it was a narrow class preserve. Audience *and* writers, I suspect, were part of an Establishment which was characterized by ghastly good-taste, gentility, and doctorates — an Anglican world of pianoforte and good posture with attachments to Empire and 'Beauty'.

The year before *Flying a Red Kite* was published, W. O. Mitchell published *Jake and the Kid*; these two books beautifully represent voices from two different worlds. It would not be unfair to say that the sensibility behind *Jake and the Kid* remains to this day the more popular and dominant.

(A *potpourri* of that dominant sensibility: W. P. Kinsella, Indian "art", Inuit "art", William Kurelek, landscape with old barn.)

The reputations of MacLennan, Callaghan, Garner, Ross, and Mitchell seem, if anything, to have grown even larger in the intervening years. Reputations in Canada take years to build and then, once built, stand copper-clad for ever like vast CN Hotels.

I'm not criticizing writers older than myself to be unpleasant or controversial. I would hope that by now I'm not really *being* controversial. We are mired at the moment in hopeless dishonesty about our literature. It's necessary to put these writers who have grossly inflated reputations in Canada into some sort of critical perspective, to compare them with their contemporaries in the rest of the English-speaking world. If this task is not undertaken by responsible critics, the lies will continue to be propagated and we will all sink beneath the burden of absurdity. We must not forget that one of the critical fraternity has already produced an explication of Garner's mindless *oeuvre*.

My interest in this is not totally disinterested. If we cannot honestly evaluate the past, we cannot make intelligent judgements about the present. As a working writer, I'm terrified of having what tiny audience there is put to sleep by the charismatic fans of Frederick Philip Grove. If I were a bright young student instructed by the owner of a Ph.D. that the works of Callaghan, Garner, and Grove were of great interest and literary importance, I'd be happy to reject CanLit forever in favour of a frisbee.

There have been attempts over the last few years to assert a native Canadian tradition in short story writing. David Arnason claims in his *Nineteenth Century Canadian Stories* that the Canadian story can be considered as "the development of the Letter to the Editor as a specialized literary form". Wayne Grady in his preface to *The Penguin Book of Canadian Short Stories*, following Arnason, suggests that the characteristic feature of Canadian stories — realism — is inherited from pioneer journalism.

Grady's preface seems to suggest — vaguely, tenuously — that Richler, Hood, Margaret Laurence, and Alice Munro somehow stand in some sort of obscure relationship to letter writers to the *Daily Stump and Stone Picker*. Common sense alone would suggest that this is nonsense.

It's interesting to read what Raymond Knister wrote of this alleged tradition in his introduction to the anthology *Canadian Short Stories* published in 1928:

> The short story has shared in the disadvantages of other types of literature and of culture as a whole in Canada. It is vain to say that it might have sprung from the soil as a new variant of the traditional form. There has been no national Burbank to create a Canadian subspecies of the short story as there was to breed Marquis wheat. It emerged, as the short story in the United States did, in a spirited emulation at best, or a shallow imitativeness at worst, of foreign models.

I would assert that the interesting story writers in Canada are writing in the world tradition of the "modern"; others would assert that the *interesting* writers are working in the tradition of the "post-modern". The revisionist attempt to create an indigenous literary tradition is damaging in two ways; it's damaging to the obvious truth and it's damaging to CanLit's future because the monuments of this spurious tradition are so ineffably boring that only the dullest of students will endure them. And it is these sons of dullness who will go on in future generations to cast the blight of their scholarship over other appalling hacks who will in turn join the pantheon of the Canadian literary great.

The federal government has recently granted a million dollars to pay for the preparation of standard texts of some of this early Canadian fascination; it's obvious before the project has even got under way that they'll only get shot of these volumes by donating sets of them to remote Indian bands and to non-English-speaking visiting dignitaries. What's depressing, though, is that a million dollars equals entrenchment.

Grady's claim in his preface to *The Penguin Book of Canadian Short Stories* that "realism" is the characteristic feature of Canadian stories may be historically accurate but to cite specifically the writing of Alice Munro, Hugh Hood, and Margaret Laurence as examples of realism seems to me to reveal an inability to read. Or it may be that the determination to hold an untenable thesis is causing him to read what he wishes to read.

Alice Munro, for example, is not a "realist"; she is a marvellously *poetic* writer. She is no mere recorder of surfaces. Her "realism" is like that of one of her favourite painters — Edward Hopper. The experience of *reading aloud* the first few paragraphs of, say, "Walker Brothers Cowboy" or "Images" should be enough to persuade even dim readers that Alice Munro is, to borrow a term, a very *painterly* writer.

Similarly, it is a profound mistake to think of Hood as a "realist". He is obsessively concerned with names, distances, weights, colours, and procedures — but he is not a "realist". Hood had, in his first book, mastered the "modern" short story and indeed had started to go beyond the confines of the "classical" epiphany story. A careful reading of "Silver Bugles, Cymbals, Golden Silks" reveals his early brilliance. Since then, Hood's work in the short story has been continually innovative and experimental. The deceptive surface "realism" of *Around the Mountain* conceals work of incredible complexity; the only critics who have begun to grapple with Hood's short fiction are Kent Thompson and Robert Lecker. Those stories which have been described as 'journalistic' or 'documentary' are not at all what they might appear to be; the stories are deeply revolutionary, radically different from anything ever written in Canada or indeed anywhere else in the world. In all of Hood's work the mundane and the eternal intersect and coexist; in Hood's world, God manifests Himself unto us in a variety of surprising and unlikely things. Hood has largely abandoned the flash and filigree of his earliest rhetoric because, I should imagine, his mastery of it bored him and because he is working a new kind of rhetoric whose austerity seems to him better suited to the largeness of his themes.

This whole question of an indigenous literary tradition is merely nationalism in a literary guise. The reinvention of the past is bad enough but critics are also inventing the shape of the present.

It's unfortunate that our literature is so precarious that were it not for the universities and, to a lesser extent, the schools, the whole house of cards might well collapse. It is unfortunate that contemporary work is so quickly seized on by universities and turned into 'courses'. The strong, and understandable, desire for Canadian masterworks *creates* masterworks; the critical judgements made are almost bound to be unbalanced. Writers quickly become entrenched; they become the "property" of those academics who dared champion them. Responsible criticism is soon seen almost as blasphemy. Such a situation applies to Mordecai Richler, Margaret Laurence, Margaret Atwood, and Robertson Davies. The old pattern is being repeated. In my own case, the inadequacies of my novels are not as widely criticized as they should be while the felicities of my stories seem largely ignored.

It would be preferable that contemporary writing were not taught at all, but if the universities and colleges withdrew their interest writing probably would not survive. Critical buffoonery can flourish only because the literary base is so narrow. It is a vaguely remembered dream to suggest that time and the Common Reader will winnow out the wheat.

But I am getting wildly ahead of myself.

As the sixties progressed, things were happening beneath the obvious surface. Story writers were scribbling away and publishing in the largely unknown little magazines, writers whose names were unknown then and are not much better known now: Hugh Hood, Clark Blaise, Alice Munro, Dave Godfrey, Ray Smith, David Helwig, Kent Thompson, Shirley Faessler, Audrey Thomas, etc. Weaver's *Tamarack Review* and *The Fiddlehead* under the editorship of Kent Thompson were alive with exciting work. I can remember listening to CBC *Anthology* one night and hearing Alice Munro's "Images"; I was envious, excited, and amazed.

Blaise's first publication in book form was in 1968, Godfrey's in 1967 and 1968, mine in 1969 and 1970, Ray Smith's in 1969, Alice Munro's in 1968. Hugh Hood's second book of short fiction appeared in 1967.

(It's worth noting that the powers that be, or were, at *The Ryerson Press* thought it prudent to have *Dance of the Happy Shades* introduced to the public in a foreword by Hugh Garner — rather like having an exhibition catalogue of Edward Hopper introduced by Norman Rockwell.)

In 1972 Margaret Atwood published *Survival* which did a lot for nationalism and the idea of a Canadian literature but which probably set *literary* appreciation back by a decade.

The literary flowering of the seventies was under way. Quite simply, this 'revolution' was the writing of people who had absorbed the far earlier revolution of the 'modern' and were writing within *its* tradition. This simple fact was sometimes obscured by the nationalist sentiments of the leaders of the movement. Dave Godfrey, for example, might have *liked* to have been writing in some indigenous tradition but his work is derived from obvious foreign models and his training as a writer was at the hands of the running dogs at Iowa.

It's interesting to consider the influx of "foreigners" at this period and their impact not only on Canadian writing but on the Canadian literary world. The list is impressive: Kent Thompson, Audrey Thomas, Jane Rule, Austin Clarke, Leon Rooke, Clark Blaise, Chris Scott, John Mills, Sonny Ladoo, Leo Simpson, etc. Our expatriates, too, funnelled in the winds of change: Mavis Gallant, Norman Levine, Dave Godfrey, Margaret Laurence, and Mordecai Richler.

There has been for years a resentment against the "foreign-ness" of some of these people — even if they are, in fact, Canadian citizens. The literary renaissance was international in style but narrowly nationalist in sentiment. I will very soon have lived more than half my life in Canada but I still arouse hostilities in certain quarters less for my behaviour than for the fact that I am not native-born. In 1977 Clark Blaise and I edited an anthology of Canadian stories called *Here and Now*. We wished to put together a book which illustrated the strengths of the Canadian story and the gains made in the seventies. Our introduction concluded: "We have not defined a literature because the litera-ture is still defining itself". Not, I would have thought, a wildly provocative statement. Canadian writer Peter Such, who was born in England, reviewed the book, snottily, and described Blaise as an American and me as an Englishman. We are, in fact, Canadian. I wrote to the *Toronto Star* in an attempt to get them to print an apology on the grounds that "Englishman", in the context, and under the provisions of the Ontario Human Rights Code, was a racially abusive epithet. They were not persuaded by the brilliance of my argument.

I agonized a great deal over becoming a Canadian citizen. While I had no wish to return to England, I had been born and formed there and had a deep love of the country and its history. But as the years passed and I found myself with a Canadian wife and a Canadian daughter I found growing within me a genuine and deep attachment to Canada and its future. I finally became a citizen in 1970.

It was a quintessentially Canadian transaction.

I knew nothing of the procedures for becoming a citizen other than that I thought that one was supposed to know the words to "O Canada" and was supposed to be able to answer questions about the political system. And it may well have been that I was confusing all this with movies about the u.s.a. and Ellis Island. But I was *emotionally* prepared. I was willing, if such a radical step were demanded, to foreswear allegiance to the Queen and the heirs of her body forever. I gathered together all my bits of paper and found the correct federal institution on Dorchester Street in Montreal — a building only slightly less brutal than a British Labour Exchange.

I was directed into a cubicle and stood facing an official who was writing on some forms. While I waited, I ran a mental check over the names of the provinces, provincial capitals, the sequence of the Great Lakes, etc. I rehearsed the names and portfolios of the current cabinet. An old Greek in the next bull-pen was attempting to deal in broken English with a very French-Canadian and was in danger of having his name entered as that of the boat on which he'd arrived.

My official took out a clean form and said,

"Do you 'ave a passport?"

"Yes."

"Nationality?"

"British."

"What is de number?"

He wrote it on the form.

"Sign here."

I signed.

"That," he said, "will cost you twelve dollar."

In my editing of *Best Canadian Stories* I've paid little attention to the exact legal status of the writers I've published. It's enough for me that they are here. For example, I have no idea whether Elizabeth Spencer is a Canadian citizen. She has lived in Montreal for many years and occasionally writes stories with a Canadian setting. If faced with two stories by Elizabeth Spencer, one set in the Southern States and one set in Montreal, I wouldn't automatically favour the one set in Montreal. I'd select the better of the two.

While I would describe myself as an ardent Canadian nationalist, I have little time for narrow nationalist concerns *in literature*; history has dictated that writing in English transcends national boundaries. It was to England's credit, and *great* advantage, that the British literary world did not say, "Yanks Go Home!" to Henry James and T. S. Eliot. Or complain that Kipling wrote about *India*. Or spurn Conrad's Polack origins. Or reject the woggishness of V. S. Naipaul.

Canada finds it more difficult to be tolerant and welcoming.

The modern story in English was shaped by the work of writers from the U.S.A., Ireland, and New Zealand. The sensibility of the English-speaking world may next be shaken and transformed by someone from Hong Kong or Belize. Or even Moose Jaw. Who knows? Closed-shop cultural policies in literature — and in any of the arts — can only lead us back into the mediocrity from which we've recently struggled. It is not totally unlikely that fine Canadian writing in the future will link us with India and Vietnam, Germany, Poland, Italy and Portugal. This is a prospect that I can only consider reasonable and pleasing.

Canadian literature is a young and tender plant in need of nurture but over the last ten years I've come to believe that any form of protectionism does more harm than good. I've come to believe that the remorselessly logical and crisp economic arguments of quota, subsidy, distribution, and tariff, are a dangerous delusion. Literature is not oil or auto parts. Our response to our literature is *our* problem. We will win by winning hearts and minds. I have seen the enemy and the enemy is not the economic might of the U.S.A. or the cultural power of England.

The Enemy is Us.

In 1971, David Helwig and Tom Marshall edited a story anthology for *Oberon* entitled *Fourteen Stories High*. This was followed in 1972 by an anthology called *New Canadian Stories* which became the title of the series which was to follow. David Helwig resigned from editing the series in 1975 because he had accepted a job with the CBC Drama Department which precluded outside work and I was offered the job as co-editor with Joan Harcourt.

The policy of the series when I took over was to publish previously unpublished work. Helwig had started the series with the intention of providing another outlet for new work and new writers. Joan Harcourt and I were receiving manuscripts by the hundred. Nearly all of them were atrocious. I was soon driven to begging friends for unpublished stories — and at that, I wasn't getting the cream because *Oberon* could not afford to match the payments offered by some of the magazines, nominal though they were. It dawned on me slowly that we were in direct competition with the literary magazines for a very small crop of good work. There was not much point in this and I began to get restless with the whole policy and purpose of the series.

Although Joan and I got on well together, I began to hanker after the idea of a fresh co-editor, someone not quite so *nice* as Joan, someone harsher in judgement. I decided on Clark Blaise. Joan resigned by mutual agreement in 1977 and I persuaded Michael Macklem, *Oberon*'s publisher, to change both the title and policy of the anthology.

The title was now to be *Best Canadian Stories* and the policy was to concentrate on republishing the best stories from the literary magazines. I *had* wanted an outright policy of republication but Macklem persuaded me that such a policy would be bad PR and would result in reviewers berating *Oberon* for closing off yet another publishing outlet. Under pressure, I agreed that we would continue to read and consider unsolicited manuscripts. When the first *Best* appeared, reviewers lamented and berated anyway even though five of the ten writers in the volume were new and young.

I'm still uncomfortable about the policy because I think there are sufficient literary magazines to provide a home for good work. These magazines do not represent an Establishment or an Orthodoxy; there are magazines which cater to every literary taste from dodo to Dada. Most of the magazines, however, are eclectic and their editors are dedicated and avid for new talent of whatever stripe. If a story writer can't get published in a Canadian literary magazine, I'm prepared to believe there's probably something wrong with his writing.

I also believe that the period the young writer spends

battering at the literary gates is strengthening; during this period when the gatekeepers seem to be deaf he will possibly come to see for himself some of the flaws and shortcomings in his work. If he goes away from the gates sore of heart and fist never to return, then that, too, is to his advantage.

I would *like* to be able to watch young writers establishing their credentials in the literary magazines over a period of a couple of years before accepting them for *Best Canadian Stories* but such a policy would be unrealistic at the moment; we have problems enough finding ten first-rate stories in any year without setting up additional hurdles.

Joan Harcourt, in her farewell introduction to the 1978 book, said:

> I learned some things during my stint as co-editor of *New* (now *Best*) *Canadian Stories*, many of them small, some that I didn't want to know, but learn I did. Mostly I learned that this country is full of people shrouded in arctic light, trapped in their Canadian loneliness, sometimes writing badly about it, sometimes well, occasionally brilliantly. Probably I've read as many stories typed on kitchen tables in efficiency apartments and in echoing old houses in small towns as has anyone in the country. Some of the writers whose stories I read cut slightly ridiculous figures, but they were fighting the battle the best way they knew. Courage is where you find it, and I do dignify them with the title 'writer' even when the stories were less than good: they had a faith and that's more important than the product.
>
> I think I learned that there is little real fiction in Canada. What we have instead are personal histories with the names changed and the facts slightly bent. .... [T]he large run of the stories we received presented carefully crafted reliquaries, little boxes in which were enshrined little memories. Some of these reliquaries were elaborately enamelled, but mostly they were simple, sturdy constructions.

This extract from her introduction illustrates what I meant when I said that Joan was *nice*. I have no disagreement with her second paragraph except that I found the "constructions" less "carefully crafted" than she did.

(Mavis Gallant, in a letter, described them disdainfully as "pallid little 'I' stories" though she was talking about the ones we'd *selected*.)

It is with Joan's first paragraph that I am in violent disagreement.

"... they had a faith and that's more important than the product."

No!

Although Joan is saying this of *inadequate* writers, it's an attitude which has condoned and fostered the mediocrity of *all* Canadian writing from its beginnings to the present.

When I was small and aunts for my birthday gave me socks, my mother used to say to my disgruntled little self, 'It's the thought that counts'. I considered this argument but it seemed to me that what I was left with was, inescapably, *socks*.

My desire to change the title and direction of *New Canadian Stories* was prompted by a belief that "product" was more important than "faith".

I was tired of socks.

It was not until 1977-78 that I felt our story writing was generally strong enough to dare, in emulation of Martha Foley's book, the new title. The manuscripts flooding in were a constant reminder that the fight for excellence was by no means won and that only the thin red rejection-slip was holding off the positive hordes of ink-stained savages. At any given moment, there are hundreds of writers in Canada writing short stories that begin:

Pig-Eye Pete and the boys were shooting the breeze out back with a six-pack of Bud and . . .

Best has only been going a few years and it has not yet taught the lessons of technique and sophistication that I hope will eventually be learned. The anthology must be seen in context. It is still a young venture and it mustn't be forgotten that it is only a *very* few years ago that Garner's crudities were highly valued. It mustn't be forgotten that the anthology sells only 2000 copies in a good year. I would regard the anthology and what it stands for as being still in an embattled position. Squat, unblinking, ready to engulf and absorb it leaving not a trace, sits the vast warty toad of Canadian taste. The most popular writers of stories in Canada are not Mavis Gallant, Alice Munro, Margaret Laurence, and Hugh Hood. The most popular writers of stories are W. P. Kinsella and W. D. Valgardson. It is salutory to remember this.

Kinsella's stories about Indians sell in their thousands. The stories are, for the most part, bad. His Indians are basically a racist creation in the sense that they speak fractured English but are graced with poetic perceptions denied to the insensitive white men — that is, they're relatively noble savages with shining teeth and a natural sense of rhythm. Kinsella writes these stories somewhat cynically, I am sure, because he is talented and has written much better stories on non-Indian themes. The second most popular writer of stories in Canada is W. D. Valgardson. Many academic critics — and even the usually lucid George Woodcock — consider him as one of the three or four best story writers in the country. I profoundly disagree. I find his writing crudely drawn and *thin*. I recently re-read all his work when I was compiling an anthology for school children; I was appalled to discover that there was not a single story that was not suitable.

Were these two writers merely popular, the fact would not be worth mentioning; what is worth stressing is that they are accepted as important literary writers by a surprising number of academic critics and literary anthologists. There is no critical consensus in Canada about Canadian writing and very little critical writing worth the paper it's printed on. I harbour the suspicion that many academic critics in English know as much about fiction as I do about nuclear fission. The situation of *Best Canadian Stories* is, at best, precarious.

Under the headline, *Required: Boldness*, Anthony Dawson reviewed *80: Best Canadian Stories* in *Canadian Literature*.

Anthologies do not simply respond to what's going on, they aren't merely repositories. They help to shape a national culture, to formulate a sense of what can or should be done by collecting the best of what has been done. But this brings up the issue of *choice*, and the responsibility for their choices that the editors must assume. And related to this is the problem of context and purpose. Bringing together diverse pieces needs to be done with an eye on the context so created, which in turn raises the question of why such a context should be created. If the anthologies are to be culturally as well as commercially successful, their editors have to face this problem boldly, and not, as seems the case with the books under review, just gather material that they happen to like; rather, they have to use the material to reflect, if not a vision, at least more than a glimpse of cultural reality.

I feel that I've *had* "more than a glimpse" of cultural reality in the last seven years of editing *New* and *Best Canadian Stories* and it's not a vision one would wish to dwell on. An attentive reading of Dawson's review left me with a pain between the eyes; I simply didn't understand what he was getting at though I was tantalized by feeling that it might be something important.

I don't really know what he means by "cultural reality". If he means, 'our culture as it really is', I could put together a book that reflected *that* from one week's rejected manuscripts. But I suspect that isn't what he means. I'm made uncomfortable by his assertion that editors should "use the material to reflect . . . cultural reality". I wouldn't want to "use" stories for anything. I don't think of stories as "material".

Could it be that by "reflect . . . a vision" he means selecting stories that together promote something? National unity, perhaps? Canadian identity? The importance of the North? The Westward shift of power? Or can he possibly mean that editors should promote a particular *kind* of writing?

I can understand editing an anthology to promote a particular *school* of writers and writing — such as the 'Movement' anthologies in England or the 'Fugitive' anthologies in the southern States — but it would surely be immoral to edit an *annual* anthology with the title *Best* from some narrowly partisan point of view? I have always insisted on working with a co-editor precisely because I'm aware of blind spots and prejudices and feel that another sensibility is a safeguard against imposing my purely personal taste — and lack of it.

I had always thought Blaise, Rooke, and I *had* a vision. That vision is simply one of excellence. We're arrogant enough to believe that we can recognize excellence but we're not arrogant enough to assert that there's only one kind. I'd contend that an annual gathering of excellence *does* shape a national culture and does formulate "a sense of what can or should be done". It stands, annually, as a beacon against the general dark.

We do not, of course, operate with the conscious burden of formulating a national culture. How unbelievably pompous and deluded we would be if we imagined any such thing possible. That Seal of Approval approach to Culture has always struck me as comically Gallic. We're simply concerned with finding ten good stories which stand up to re-readings. It's impossible to "formulate" a national culture whatever the Liberal Government may think to the contrary. That's the sort of loopy bureaucratic idea that emerges from slow Fridays at Secretary of State. Our national culture will eventually be found to be, quite simply, the sum of individual excellences.

Dawson goes on to say:

> *80: Best Canadian Stories* has at least the unity provided by its exhibition of a single genre, and the influence the series has had on the development of that genre over the past 10 years has undoubtedly been significant, although it may not have been entirely beneficial. Judging by the present, anniversary volume, the boundaries of the genre do not seem to have been extensively tested or expanded. Excepting 'Speck's Idea,' the selection is rather drab, predictable, cautious, though there is some deft work by newcomers Martin Avery, Linda Svendsen, and Guy Vanderhaege. As a whole, the volume has not been sufficiently *built* around its impressive centrepiece.

My general reaction to this kind of flatulence is to wish that I could rub the reviewer's nose in the mountains of manuscript and mounds of magazines I trudge through every year. Dawson — and others with similar complaints — surely *must* be aware that editors of annual anthologies *can't* "build" what they might *like* to "build". They are obviously restricted to the stories published in any given year. I do agree that it would be lovely if we had ten writers as good as Mavis Gallant each of whom published new work every year and each of whom agreed to its republication for the nominal sum that *Oberon* can afford to offer. But such is not the case.

Dawson is not alone in thinking our selections "drab, predictable, cautious". Some reviewer or another has described every single volume as "conservative". Perhaps all these reviewers are aware of wild and innovative stories which have escaped our attention entirely for years. In the book Dawson is discussing there appears the story by drab, cautious, old Leon Rooke entitled "Sixteen-Year-Old Susan March Confesses to the Innocent Murder of All the Devious Strangers Who Would Drag Her Down" — as weird a piece of scrivening as one would find in a day's march. But perhaps, as the grumpy millennial leader in the *Beyond the Fringe* skit says, perhaps I'm *very* old fashioned.

Something I've noticed over the last few years is the way that new writers are seized on and then quickly discarded. Fashion meets CanLit. Boring old Alice Munro, positively antiquated old Hood. Of course, few people have managed to read either very carefully. Soon, I have no doubt, Rooke will be consigned to the rear shelves as a toothless mumbler and Hodgins will be issued his walking-stick. Such blasé attitudes in so short a span of years — as though all these critics and reviewers are operating ahistorically entirely unaware or forgetful of the fact that it was *only fourteen years ago* that it was felt necessary to use Hugh Garner to introduce the revolutionary new Alice Munro.

It could be argued, I suppose, that this desire for the new, non-drab, and unpredictable, illustrates the distance we've travelled in fourteen years and is welcome evidence of a new literary sophistication sweeping the land. The only problem with such a claim is that, in my experience at least, readers simply do not fully understand even the earliest of Alice Munro's stories. Her work has suffered at the hands of dim feminists who have quarried it for ammunition and who have, inevitably, diminished it as literature. When Alice Munro turned out not to be a prophet of escalating sexual violence or indeed a propagandist of any sort, the more volatile in her following drifted away. All this, of course, had little to do with Alice; she simply continued writing stories which was all she'd been interested in doing in the first place. The quest for the fashionably new continues; it is not a literary quest.

Some jaded reviewer can always be relied upon to drag in the avant-garde. Why, they cry, doesn't *Best Canadian Stories* feature the work of x or y? Some reviewers see *Best* as an Establishment anthology but how they manage to do so when it has an open-arms policy to talent and regularly prints the work of young newcomers writing in any style baffles me. I wish I had the leather chair and decanter of port to go with the reputation.

(Cockburn '92 is always mentioned respectfully if anyone's in a donating mood.)

Why doesn't *Best* publish the avant-garde? The best answer I can give is to quote a review I wrote in 1975 of the avant-garde anti-Establishment anthology *The Story So Far 3* published by *The Coach House Press.* It must be understood that this review does not necessarily reflect the views of my co-editor, Leon Rooke, some of whose own work is capable of causing the eyebrow to rise.

This anthology of twenty-five short stories is the third in what threatens to become an annual event. The contents of the book might be described as antiquarian avant-garde. The titles of some of the offerings indicate the nauseating pretensions of the whole — 'scenario for a comicbook', 'three untitled pieces', 'Counting Combinations — a legend of partial distance'. No doubt we are dealing here with Art.

Many of the pieces are free from such conformist conventions as orthodox spelling and punctuation. Those which are not entirely liberated indulge mainly in ellipsis.

'And now I begin. I rub . . . I push . . . So hard . . . So humid No, don't touch me . . . wait, not now.'

Oh, God . . .

George Bowering who describes himself as 'living and writhing' in Vancouver is still addicted to the ampersand.

It saddened me to see Terry Heath in such company; he published a good book in 1972 entitled *The Truth and Other Stories.* Daphne Marlatt is capable of better things. Matt Cohen is vastly more gifted than the present sample would indicate.

I was intrigued to encounter A. S. A. Harrison again if only because she edited an unintentionally comic master-piece (also for the Coach House coterie) entitled *Twenty-two Women Talk Frankly About Their Orgasms.* I was immensely taken with the acknowledgements in that book. They read, in part, *I am grateful to the women who granted me interviews, including Pascal, Granada, Rosy, Angela, whose orgasms are not included here.*

The piece that appealed to me most was "The Mole" by Martin Howard Vaughn-James, inventor of the 'visual novel', because it contained only sixty-one words. I was grateful, too, for George Bowering's maunderings because the funny spelling reminded me of Ring Lardner and I went back to "The Young Immigrunts" which contains the lines:

Are you lost daddy I arsked tenderly
Shut up he explained.

The book is illustrated with photographs of the authors who present brief autobiographical and bibliographical credentials:

Noddy McCoy 'had a nervous breakdown at the top of the Torre del Mangia, Siena. She does not cook or sew'.

Gerry Gilbert 'writes in the dark' and 'squats to crap'.

Steve McCaffery 'aetat 4: imagained a colour to be black. practised 'a secret thing'. aetat 8: attempted to see a pot, trebled it, read gertrude stein aetat 24'.

It's all very sad isn't it?

The book was funded by the Canada Council.

There are hundreds of aspiring writers in Canada and I have read the work of most of them; it has had permanent effects on my disposition. Since *New Canadian Stories* became *Best Canadian Stories*, the flood of manuscripts has slowed, thank God, to a trickle. This is pleasing for two reasons. First, I don't have to wade through five stories a week that begin: *Brrr! The alarm-clock . . . .* Second, it suggests that *Best*'s growing reputation has percolated right down even to the hardcore literasts who had previously submitted, repeatedly, stories and even articles they had originally had published in their parish magazines in 1924.

My years of experience led me to formulate four general rules about unsolicited manuscripts which I am willing to pass on for the edification of those who might in the future become involved in editorial work.

1) *Any unsolicited manuscript sent by Registered Mail or Special Delivery will turn out to be peculiarly awful.*

2) Many manuscripts arrive in folders, glassine binders, or pastel dockets or are secured with intricate clips and clamps, or are bound by gay ribbons. Many of these manuscripts are introduced by several pages of front matter — title page, half-title, epigraph etc. — often on paper of contrasting colours.

The fancier the package, the worse the contents.

3) *Manuscripts tend to be ghastly in proportion to the order and number of the following notations found on the title page:*

   (a) *The number of the words to the nearest thousand.*

   (b) *The number of words to the nearest hundred.*

   (c) *The exact number of words.*

   (d) *North American Serial Rights Only.*

   (e) *A circle containing the letter c in indication of copyright.*

   If a title page bears (c), the manuscript is bad. If a title page bears (c), (d), and (e), the manuscript should be returned unread.

4) There is a surprising number of aspirants who seem convinced that their work is likely to be plagiarized by the mailman.

   Those authors who are most obviously paranoid about copyright are those with the least cause for anxiety.

I'm not an excessively formal person but it irritates me to receive letters on square bits of paper headed: Memo From The Desk Of. Some correspondents favour Holiday Inn stationery. Others write on elaborate letterhead which incorporates their photograph and advertises their other artistic ventures such as Pastel Portraiture and Scissor Silhouettes. Some authors, invariably female, decorate their letters with magic marker flowers and Happy Faces.

Salutations, too, often depart from convention:

"Dear Oberon,"

"Dear Eds"

"Hello there!"

"Hi!"

It may be of sociological interest that letters which begin "Hi!" are always from women, are usually decorated with Happy Faces or flowers, *and are invariably from British Columbia.*

Many authors include a curriculum vitae which details volunteer work in hospitals and lists their prior publications in *Container and Contents* — the house organ of the Canadian Reinforced Cardboard Box Company.

More than one covering letter has resorted to emotional blackmail describing recent open-heart surgery and suggesting that acceptance of the enclosed would speed recovery . . .

It is sometimes hard to keep alive the necessary faith and enthusiasm for this task, hard to keep in mind that it is a project that by its nature must take years to bear fruit abundantly.

In one manuscript, adhering to, almost *fused* with, was an uncooked hamburger.

The twenty years that have passed since my arrival in Canada have seen vast changes in our literature. At first glance, the difference between 1962 and 1982 is like the difference between desert and oasis. There are more writers and better writers. Some six or seven bookstores specialize in Canadian books and most bookstores, with the exception of the large chains, carry a passable selection of Canadian fiction. The Canada Council buys its own products and donates them generously. Going to or returning from a public reading of one's work, it is impossible not to bump into fellow-writers in airports.

If forced to generalities, I'd say that the strongest genre in Canada is the short story and the weakest the novel. It would not be realistic to hope for more than one major poet in any fifty year period. In any country. Our two most important poets are Irving Layton and John Newlove but it's far too early to assess their achievement. I suspect that the idea of a "major poet" — one who changes our emotional landscape and recharges our language — is now an historical concept; impact requires audience and poetry has become dangerously marginal. The sensibility and manner of our best story writers is basically poetic and it may well be that there is something about our times that prompts people who might once have written poetry to write prose instead.

There has been a blurring of the lines between poetry and prose for some sixty years now; Hemingway's brief "vignettes" which separate the stories in *In Our Time* are more concentratedly poetic than most verse since. The opening paragraphs of Katherine Mansfield's "Miss Brill" rise above the normal rhythms of conventional prose into something more highly charged. The verse, on the other hand, of both Hemingway and Katherine Mansfield is unbelievable inept and embarrassing.

Odd.

Where twenty years ago Canadian stories stressed content — what a story was *about* — the main emphasis now is on the story as verbal and rhetorical *performance*. Our best writers are concerned with the story as *thing to be experienced* rather than as *thing to be understood*. This more than anything else is what seems to baffle some readers — and not a few critics; it is difficult for those of us writing stories to understand why this is so since these concerns have been dominant since about 1920.

In an essay that Alice Munro wrote for me this year for a book I was editing, she said:

> I will start out by explaining how I read stories written by other people. For one thing, I can start reading them anywhere; from beginning to end, from end to beginning, from any point in between in either direction. So obviously I don't take up a story and follow it as if it were a road, taking me somewhere, with views and neat diversions along the way. I go into it, and move back and forth and settle here and there, and stay in it for a while. It's more like a house. Everybody knows what a house does, how it encloses space and makes connections between one enclosed space and another and presents what is outside in a new way. This is the nearest I can come to explaining what a story does for me, and what I want my stories to do for other people.

The implications of this paragraph alone should be enough to give pause to those who consider Alice Munro a simple "realist". What she says here is very like some notes for school children I wrote in 1980 for a junior high school text called *New Worlds*:

"The 'What does it mean?' approach to the story could be compared with the package-tour traveller who 'does' Europe or Africa in fourteen days. I suggest settling down in a place, learning the language, observing the ways of the inhabitants until you begin to understand their world."

It's probably a very dangerous analogy to make because painting and writing really cannot be compared but the changes in the short story in Canada over the last twenty years are not wildly unlike the changes in painting at a slightly earlier period. I'd suggest that the story pre-1962 could be compared with traditional representative painting and that the changes since have moved the story closer to an equivalent of abstraction. Though it's precisely there that the analogy collapses — for words have meanings. I don't mean to suggest by 'abstraction' that the modern story lacks immediate reference to the external world. Obviously not. I mean rather that formal concerns are becoming increasingly important.

It possibly makes little sense and sheds no light but the Canadian painter with whom I, for example, tend to identify immediately is David Milne. His concerns in the watercolours and drypoints seem to me exactly the sort of things that I'm trying to do with words.

Our major story writers are Mavis Gallant, Norman Levine, Hugh Hood, Alice Munro, Leon Rooke, and Clark Blaise. Of these writers, Levine and Rooke are the ones most obviously concerned with rhetoric and form. Rooke is writing in a relatively contemporary American tradition, Levine in an older American, now international, tradition. In 1972 when I seemed to know more than I do now, I wrote the following review of *I Don't Want To Know Anyone Too Well* for *The Canadian Forum*.

The fifteen stories in Norman Levine's new collection explore loss of youth, loneliness, varieties of failure, and death, and express a stoicism in the face of these adversities. Nearly all the stories are constructed in much the same way – an incident or a memory is recounted, usually in the first person, and the events are put down one after the other in almost reportorial fashion. The end of the story is usually off-hand, seemingly casual, determinedly flat.

The end of 'A True Story' illustrates the manner. The story recounts the beginnings of a hoped-for affair and ends with the girl's sudden death. On his way back from the funeral, the narrator meets a colleague.

'Isn't it a glorious day,' he said.

'It is,' I said.

The sun was shining. The snow on the ground glistened.

We could see our breath in the cold air.

In other words, Levine is writing text-book examples of 'the modern short story.'

A typical Hemingway story, 'The End of Something' finishes:

'Have a scene?'

'No, there wasn't any scene.'

'How do you feel?'

'Oh, go away, Bill! Go away for a while.'

Bill selected a sandwich from the lunch basket and walked over to have a look at the rods.

But that was in 1923.

The determinedly flat is, of course, as much a piece of rhetoric as is the final speech of a corpse-strewn Elizabethan play; the fact that we can recognize and discuss it as a device shows us that it, too, is an *historical* rhetoric.

When the device succeeds, it can still produce moving work. Levine more than succeeds with such stories as 'A Small Piece of Blue', 'By the Richelieu', 'My Wife Has Left Me', 'A Canadian Upbringing', and 'South of Montreal'. These stories are haunting. In each of them certain details are so fictionally right that they are unforgettable — the alcoholic doctor at the northern mine who ritually shoots at a candle-flame with an air rifle in his office; Marsden, the exile and ex-writer, who makes toy roundabouts. Yet even in these most successful stories, an invisible worm eats away at one's pleasure.

One is always aware of Hemingway's looming bulk and sadly aware that such stories in 1971 are a cliché; the pattern of their rhetoric is predictable. I know; I've written them myself.

Just as some people are trapped and made rigid by some concept of 'good breeding', so Levine is trapped in a delicate but out-moded form. That form no longer delivers the poetry. There is no point now in writing Joyce novels or rhyming couplets. Levine is writing superbly within what is now a formula. Gulley Jimson said Lady Beeder's watercolours were like 'farting Annie Laurie through a key hole. It may be clever but is it worth the trouble!'

Because Levine has not challenged himself in terms of form and style, his very mastery becomes boring — like watching Minnesota Fats playing billiards. His chasteness and perfection made me long for struggle and vulgarity.

The succeeding ten years of reading and re-reading have taught me that I was wrong, that Levine's rhetoric does still deliver the poetry. I've reprinted this review not only so that I could apologize for it but also because it interests me, looking back ten years, to realize how firmly I was locked into rhetorical interests.

Sophistication in style and rhetoric is now more widespread than it was even five years ago. During the last few years the general quality of story writing in the country has improved dramatically. I'm not really sure why this should be. I would like to flatter myself that *Best Canadian Stories* has played a part but this probably isn't true in the sense of its offering literary models to younger writers; it must be remembered that the best writers in the world are only as far away as a bookstore or library. Canadian writing at the moment is only a small and minor current in a very big river. *Best Canadian Stories* may have had some indirect effect, however, simply by existing and by offering evidence, perhaps imperfect, that it is possible to be Canadian *in Canada* and still be in touch with a larger sense of excellence. When our best writers publish in international magazines and are republished in *Best Canadian Stories*, it should be an encouragement to all younger writers to know that it is indeed possible to become something more than a spine with a maple leaf stuck on it.

One of the pleasures of editing *Best Canadian Stories* is in the recognition and launching of new talent. Writing, oddly enough, is not a particularly competitive business. Most writers are wise enough to know that all writing is unique and that all writers are part of a tradition which is larger and more important than personal vanities. It has given me great pleasure to be of use to writers at the beginnings of their careers. It's probably invidious to refer to particular people but I've been deeply impressed and excited by the work of Linda Svendsen and Keath Fraser; I have few doubts that they will forge important literary careers.

My hopes for the anthology are that it will come to have such a reputation that writers will consider themselves honoured to be selected. I don't intend this in any arrogant way or mean to imply that our *imprimatur* is the source of the honour; rather, that the book should become, if this makes any sense, a *communal* expression of excellence in writing. Our stance is not Olympian; we are genuinely grateful if readers and other writers draw work to our attention.

As our writing matures and we develop *more* writers of quality, it is not perhaps silly to imagine beginners here reading *Best Canadian Stories* as attentively as they should be reading *Best American Stories* and *Winter's Tales* from England. I am idealistic enough to hope that one day readers and young writers in England and the u.s.a. will look forward to the annual appearance of *Best Canadian Stories* as a normal and unremarked feature of the literary life.

Although our literature has improved beyond recognition in the last twenty years, the literary situation remains precarious. Although there are books and visible authors and although there are new young writers dedicating themselves to a life of extremely hard work with meagre rewards, there is still one huge fly in the Canadian ointment; nearly all the gains made since 1962 are reflections of the various activities of the Canada Council. The literary base is so narrow that the superstructure is ludicrously unstable. As I've said over and over again, the one thing we still lack — and it's the most important thing — is an audience. Money can subsidize the writers, the magazines, the printers, and the publishers, but an audience can't be bought.

I have no solution to the problem.

I do have vague Sunday School memories of a hymn which involved the general idea of the prevailing darkness of sin illuminated here and there by the individual candles of *good* girls and boys. The words, "You in your small corner and I in mine" somehow linger. Or possibly, "me in mine". Or perhaps that was another hymn altogether. But what I'm getting at is the power of individual points of light to dispel dark. It's an answer of sorts and Despair is a sin.

When I moved from Delta to live in Ottawa, I spent my first few weeks pottering about finding out where life's essentials were. One of my first stops was the main branch of the Ottawa Public Library. Naturally, I wanted to see how many of my books they had. Curiosity satisfied on that score, I decided to check out the situation with *Best Canadian Stories*.

"I think we'll find them," said the library lady, "under 'B' in 'Fiction in English'. Or possibly . . . "

I followed her Wallabies.

" . . . under 'W'. A very good series."

I nodded and smiled.

"I do so enjoy his historical novels."

"Pardon?"

"Here you are," she said, gesturing at a rank of familiar spines.

"Ah! Thank you," I said. "Why might they have been under 'W'?"

Spectacles decorated with rhinestone butterflies.

"They're edited," she said, "by Rudy Wiebe."

Kicking Against the Pricks

READ how the reputation-makers of Toronto's literary mafia bury those who dare oppose them. . . .

WATCH character-assassination in a bedroom in the Royal York. . . .

TREMBLE as you see the tentacles of 'their thing' reaching across the nation and around the world. . . .

The reader's closest attention is necessary if he is to grasp the twists and turns of the following infamous story. Follow the five (numbered) stages of the plot. It is a chilling tale of spite and malice, of a thirst for revenge which only remaindering can sate. . . .

I

On Saturday, January 17th, 1976, there appeared in the Montreal *Gazette* the following review:

Well-made short tales — overcast with dullness

75: New Canadian Stories

Edited by David Helwig and Joan Harcourt
Oberon Press

There used to be a rumour going around that all the books published by Oberon were actually written by its owner, Michael Macklem, who used various pseudonyms and "modes" but, alas, kept the same style, theme, and jacket design for each one.

No one really complained and it wasn't a vicious rumour, for the books were for the most part readable and inoffensive. And there was the predictability, the unattenuable sameness, that Canadians tend to identify with a tradition.

But the rumour has been disproved, and it is now believed

that Oberon is in fact a fine stable of writers in grey blankets kept and groomed for spring showings. These writers produce good, solid work on a regular basis: They write witty, urbane novels and edit quiet, well-disciplined anthologies of each other's stories. Their books are always aesthetically pleasing. No taste is left in the mouth.

In 1971, David Helwig came to Oberon and set himself the task of editing *Fourteen Stories High*. Helwig was angry, he said, at the lack of markets for new Canadian writing. He wanted to help "Make good art popular and popular art good", so he selected people for his Ark who had never seemed to have trouble finding markets before: Hugh Garner, Doug Spettigue, Phyllis Gotlieb, George Bowering, Alden Nowlan, Marian Engel. The book sold well.

It sold so well, in fact, that *Fourteen Stories High* became a series, almost an institution — although there were some changes, one of which was the title. As Helwig says in his present introduction, "the title proved a hard act to follow; we soon ran low on promising architectural metaphors and settled on the perhaps dull, but informative *72: New Canadian Stories*."

Unfortunately, the epithet "dull but informative" applied to the stories inside as well as to the title, and the criteria they settled on in '72 became the jinx they've been saddled with ever since. A pall of mediocrity has crept over the series. The stories continue to be well made and well sold, but they are overcast with a murky dullness, a kind of professional, rather than artistic, stability.

It is a sad truth that although bad writing makes a story bad by definition, good writing alone cannot make a good story. Many of Oberon's writers rely for their interest on the quality of their form, and hardly at all on the importance or impact of their content.

Joyce Marshall's 'Summer' is a case in point. It should have been a good story, but somehow it just doesn't work. Great pains are taken to recapture the atmosphere of an adolescent friendship between an omnipresent first-person and another girl. Once that has been done, however, the purpose of the story is accomplished, and the reader is dropped holding a handful of atmosphere that neither he nor the author know what to do with. The pains seem to have been taken for their own sake, not for ours, nor even for the writer's.

Marshall herself seems aware of this, for she ends the story with a kind of desperate catch-up paragraph meant to enlarge the story's dimensions, but which really abandons her original intention for a condensed novel, which a short story is not.

So David Helwig is still angry — "perhaps more so," he says, "than five years ago." We need more middlemen, "more editors, agents, producers, entrepreneurs and first-class literary journalists who combine fine minds with the instincts of a seventeenth-century buccaneer." More people, in other words, who are able to take the kinds of risks that Helwig himself was not able to take with these anthologies. Perhaps this is why Helwig is leaving Oberon and the New Canadian Stories series to work as an editor for the CBC.

While Helwig sweats it out in the fire, his place in the pan will be taken by John Metcalf, who is not your average seventeenth-century buccaneer.

WAYNE GRADY

II

On January 31st, 1976, the following letter appeared in the Montreal *Gazette* on the book-page. It was set off by a heavy black border.

Review of Oberon Book malicious, incompetent
The Book Editor,

In The Gazette on Saturday, Jan. 17, there appeared what purported to be a review by Wayne Grady of *75: New Canadian Stories* edited by David Helwig and Joan Harcourt and published by the Oberon Press. The book contains 11 stories, yet the review commented — passingly — on only one.

The review opened with an attack on the person of the publisher and owner of Oberon Press, Michael Macklem. It then proceeded to a generalized attack on all the writers on Oberon's list. Joan Harcourt, David Helwig, and the Oberon Press were then sneeringly attacked for their record over the last five years with the New Canadian Stories series of anthologies. This was

176

followed by some weighty Grade Eleven stuff of a literary nature. The review ended with the information that I had taken Helwig's place as editor and that Wayne Grady felt dubious about my abilities.

The general tone of this piece of murky Grub Street made me curious. Who was Wayne Grady and, more to the point, what was the matter with him? My curiosity got the better of me and I phoned Macklem to ask him if he had ever done something nasty to someone called Wayne Grady. It turned out, as I'd suspected from the tone of the review, that he had. The Oberon Press had rejected a novel by Wayne Grady in December 1974.

I am bothering to write these paragraphs not because Oberon was attacked, not because Macklem was attacked, not because I was attacked, but because one of the most influential papers in Canada gave over its lead review to a malicious incompetent. As a result, Montreal readers were lied to and deprived of a fair estimation of a not unimportant book.

Macklem, a gentleman of admirable restraint, merely said: "As long as we use amateur reviewers in this country, what can we expect but generalized pique?"

I was once told by a journalist in Winnipeg as we consumed beer together that on his paper book-reviews were handed out to staff journalists as punishment for dereliction of duty: five minutes late for the fire and you got 500 words on the latest novel, or worse, poetry. And I don't think he was kidding me.

Reviewing is an honourable and arduous job; it is also a full-time job. Our literature is likely to remain a frontier activity if reviewing is left in the hands of writers, failed writers, the near-literate, and people's aunts.

When the annual literary awards are announced in France riot ensues; those books which receive prizes are sold in their thousands. The announcement here of the Governor-General's Awards is decently suppressed unless someone from Quebec is rude.

We will never have a flourishing literary culture in Canada until we have professional criticism and reviewing, until newspapers assume the part they have traditionally played in civilized society.

JOHN METCALF

III

In 1976 I assumed editorship, with Joan Harcourt, of Oberon's annual *New Canadian Stories*. We were receiving and reading hundreds of stories but most of them were aggressively bad. It became obvious to me that I would have to solicit stories from writers of repute and attempt to scout out younger writers through literary magazines.

I'd seen two or three stories by a young writer called Michael Smith — I believe they were in *Canadian Fiction Magazine*. I wrote to Smith asking him if he had any unpublished work I might consider for the anthology. He sent me two or three stories which I read carefully. I thought they showed some promise but that they were not of sufficient merit to warrant inclusion. I wrote a polite and encouraging letter to Smith explaining my reactions and urging him to send me future work.

Subsequent to this correspondence, Michael Smith seemed to stop publishing stories and started to write reviews for *Books in Canada*. I have always wondered if it were pure coincidence that he was given assignments to review *The Teeth of My Father* (1976), *Girl in Gingham* (1978), and *General Ludd* (1980).

None of them won his unrestrained and wholehearted approval.

Any doubts I might have had about Smith's hostility were cleared up in 1978 when Douglas Marshall, then editor of *Books in Canada*, asked me if I'd do an interview for the magazine. Marshall was a supporter of the rather juvenile policy of bringing together oil and water and the interviewer turned out to be none other than Michael Smith.

I was staying in Toronto for a few days at the Royal York Hotel. Michael Smith phoned me and we arranged to do the interview in my hotel room. When he arrived, late, he turned out to be a small, rumpled, sweaty man. He was rather grumpy in manner and seemed to blame me for the long drive he'd had from his home town. I treated him with my usual courtesy and procured beer from Room Service to cool him down.

I have since regretted the expense.

It became obvious after a few minutes that he was attempting to lure me into what he considered indiscretions. The interview became openly hostile. What was insulting was that he seemed to imagine his ponderous stratagems opaque. Since I have nothing to hide and little to protect, it amused me to respond in exactly the way he wished. At the conclusion of the interview, I asked him politely if he would show me a transcript of the interview before it was published. This is standard practice. He seemed most reluctant but said that he would. He didn't.

The interesting part of the interview, *as published*, runs as follows.

IV

BOOKS IN CANADA: You've said elsewhere that writing has to be an aristocratic activity. I read recently in one of your books a reference to Canada being a country where green Coke bottles are considered antiques. I wonder if to be a short-story writer or a novella writer you have to write from a snobbish point of view.

METCALF: I don't find anything snobbish in intelligence. I find that the kind of remark, if you'll excuse me, that ill-educated people make about things that they don't understand. How many people read *War and Peace* as opposed to *Valley of the Dolls*? They're different productions, and they're for different audiences. If I set out to write deliberately to entertain hundreds of thousands of people I would by definition have to write rubbish. Reading — reading well — is a supremely intellectual activity, and very few people can read very well. In Canada fewer people can read well than in most other countries.

BOOKS IN CANADA: In your novella, *Private Parts*, the narrator seems similar in many ways to yourself, and yet his view of the way he's performed in the literary world is that he's a minor writer of "loneliness and self-discovery." Do the feelings you've just expressed include your own feelings about success or failure?

METCALF: Well, first of all I would draw an extreme line between any identification between John Metcalf and the narrator of *Private Parts*. In fact, in *Private Parts* the narrator is given a name that is not mine. However, yes, certainly I see myself as a minor writer for the simple reason that I compare myself, as I think every good writer should, with Shakespeare, Tolstoy, Dickens —

and when you compare yourself with people like that, nearly all of us are pretty miserable efforts.

These questions reveal either extreme literary naivety or malice.

The reference to writing being an aristocratic activity is a reference to an "essay" I wrote in *The Narrative Voice* called "Soaping a Meditative Foot: Notes for a Young Writer". The quotation reads:

"Do not confuse your politics with your writing. Party political positions are necessary in the larger world; the literary world is necessarily aristocratic".

This quotation comes from a larger context wherein I was warning young writers of the dangers of writing fiction which was political propaganda. By "aristocratic", I meant, of course, that writing concerns itself only with excellence. (The complete text can be found in *The Narrative Voice*, p. 154.)

Smith managed to distort this statement by pretending to understand "aristocratic" in a *social* sense. He then compounded this "misunderstanding" by ascribing to me a comment *made by a character in a piece of fiction* (Jim Wells in *General Ludd*, p. 27). He then "wonders" if to write short stories and novellas it is necessary to write from a snobbish point of view. "Wonder", indeed! The question finally posed asks, more or less, if I am aristocratic and snobbish.

This is low comedy of the 'Have you stopped beating your wife?' variety and the best answer, of course, would have been the back of my hand.

Michael Smith's second question is one that wouldn't have been asked by someone well-taught in Grade Ten. The form of the question ("the feelings you've just expressed" — when according to the printed transcript I've expressed none) suggests problems with the tape. I prefer to consider this identification of writer with narrator malicious rather than naive because Michael Smith is now Editor of *Books in Canada* and if it wasn't malicious we must all face up to the fact that the most widely distributed organ of literary opinion in Canada is directed by a person who is exceedingly dim about very, very basic literary distinctions.

V

The next stage in this tortuous tale of suspense and intrigue exhibits the combined talents of Smith, the Editor of *Books in Canada*, and Grady, the Managing Editor of *Books in Canada*, a team that puts me in mind of T. Sturge Moore's comment on Chesterton and Belloc — "Two buttocks of one bum".

The following extract is from an amazing piece written by Wayne Grady for the *The Tamarack Review*.

"Copeland, Valgardson, Munro, and Kinsella are regional writers whose books, like the rural communities they depict, are intricate interdependencies, each story an individual and part of a whole. Their styles are practical, even perfunctory, with few wasted words and infrequent regard for the nice philosophies of their slicker, urban counterparts, represented here by John Metcalf, David Lewis Stein, Hugh Hood, and Matt Cohen. These last do not publish books that are cohesive units trembling on the brink of being novels. Their books are not collections, but selections; they are not regional, they are cosmopolitan.

In an interview published in January's *Books in Canada*, John Metcalf characterized himself as a 'minor writer' who wanted 'to move into a blacker kind of humour, because I think the times are demanding it'. 'Private Parts', the long short story that forms the first half of *Girl in Gingham*, has been called by Irving Layton 'a goy's *Portnoy's Complaint*': a black comedy of sorts, it describes a boy's discovery of the joys and sorrows of self-abuse, which he calls 'wanking', and how he exchanges it in later life for the joys and sorrows of being a minor writer. The title story concerns a divorcé whose computer date, during a dinner date in a Montreal restaurant, suddenly and noisily dies. Since neither story is really *about* anything of consequence (an occupational hazard among urban writers) their interest relies mainly on their style, which in turn relies for its effect on an accumulation of swift detail, one-liners: characters made up entirely of traits, whole paragraphs composed of briefly observed gestures and boiled down phrases. A style, in fact, not unlike the restaurant to which Peter, the divorcé, takes Anna, his *in extrêmis* date:

'Since his last visit, to his horror, the restaurant had fallen prey to a prodigal decorator. The overall effect was of an end-of-lease sale at the premises of an unsuccessful chandler. Every nook, recess, and area of wall had been jammed, plastered, and festooned with nets, buoys, bollards, binnacles, belaying-pins, barnacle-encrusted brass bells, anchors, cutlasses, hawsers, harpoons, lanterns, strings of bunting and lengths of rusted chain.'

But that kind of restaurant *is* successful: the times are demanding it."

The reader can decide for himself if in the Smith interview I characterized myself absolutely as a minor writer or if Grady is perhaps being less than scrupulous in his employment of quotation. The reader can also decide if the review seems to offer a balanced opinion or if it is energized by a certain inexplicable animus.

And here, for the moment, this Ugly Vendetta ends.

Well, *no*.

Not quite.

There are other matters in Grady's piece which should concern and amaze those interested in literature. Only a person with a tin ear and a loose grip on logic could have written "his *in extremis* date" and only someone in dire need of a dictionary could have managed "unattenuable sameness" but I shall attempt to ignore the clumsiness of the writing and the rather personal punctuation though it goes against the grain to do so; I see no reason to pay attention to those who analyse, criticize, and explicate, if they themselves seem incapable of journeyman English.

It amazes me that Grady could consider Alice Munro's style "perfunctory"; it amazes me to realize that Grady thinks I have a "philosophy"; it amazes me that Grady seems to think Alice Munro *unslick*, if by that he means less sophisticated, less polished. It amazes me that he would even *rank* Alice Munro with Ann Copeland, Valgardson, and Kinsella.

This vision of a "regional" Alice Munro daubed with sheep-shit and with vagrant straws sticking out of her hair, a raw-boned regional lass slapping down her stories in her practical style with few wasted words is certainly not the Alice Munro *I* know. And I doubt if it's the Alice Munro who publishes regularly in *The New Yorker*.

The other three regional yoiks he mentions are university professors.

Is "regional" a good word and "cosmopolitan" a bad word? And the further the review goes, the less of it I understand.

"Since neither story is really *about* anything of consequence (an occupational hazard among urban writers) their interest relies mainly on their style . . . ."

Is Grady *seriously* saying that if one writes about events that take place in towns or cities one is likely not to be writing about anything of consequence? If this *is* what he's saying, and it seems to be, then I am rendered speechless.

His preference for content over form — as if they were divisible — and denigration of style are hopelessly hayseed and philistine; there's more straw showing than hair.

But now to remove tongue from cheek and to stop being playful. This lengthy and tedious history of a literary dispute with a *pisher* like Grady would not be important were it not for Grady's power and influence which now unfortunately extend beyond Canada. Grady has been appointed editor of two volumes of Canadian stories published by Penguin books. These books are presumably available beyond our shores and present a literary image of Canada to other countries. Needless to say, my work is not represented in them. No surprises there. But neither is the work of Clark Blaise, one of our most brilliant writers. Neither is the work of Leon Rooke, a writer of dazzling virtuosity. I hope their exclusion from these representative books is not because of their friendship and association with me. Though I probably flatter myself. On the evidence of his review in *Tamarack*, Grady is quite capable of dredging up a wild variety of bizarre literary reasons for their exclusion.

Hugh Hood, that antique "transitional" figure, was added to the book as an afterthought.

The rise of Wayne Grady to literary fame and fortune as Managing Editor of *Books in Canada* and Editor of the Penguin books of short stories is all too typical of Canadian literary life. What are his credentials? "A background in popular journalism" states one note. Which means that he wrote for *Weekend Magazine* and other such organs of opinion. Which is rather like handing over the editorship of *The Times Literary Supplement* to Dear Abby.

The two most influential figures connected with *Books in Canada* are at least failed writers. If only as much could be said of reviewers in general. During my literary career so far I have published 5⅓ books of fiction and edited some sixteen or so literary compilations which have received review. Reviews sent by publishers seem to flow across my desk almost daily. A few of these reviews, positive *and* negative, are intelligent and thoughtful. Some are competent. But a large number range from daffy to semi-literate.

The following reviews and excerpts from reviews are all of books I have written or edited over the last twelve years. I have arranged them into categories because I'm interested less in what they say about individual books than in what they reveal about reviewers and newspapers. Each review or collection of snippets is intended to represent a type and to stand for others.

The Wrong Man

I have been plagued ever since I started writing by an author called John Metcalfe. We share a parallel career. I do wish reviewers were capable of reading jackets, spines, blurbs, or title pages. Is it much to ask? The latest Metcalfe review to date was January 1982 in *The Globe and Mail*. Peter Sypnowich in the *Toronto Daily Star* in 1970 got Metcalf right but nodded off *in medias res* and started referring to me as John Newlove.

One has one's pride.

Parrot Reviews

Monty Python's Flying Circus once did a very silly skit about the Parrot News. "Twenty cars were demolished this evening in a mass pile-up on the M1. No parrots were involved . . . In the worst crash in aviation history . . . no parrots were among the victims."

Some reviews share this specialized kind of interest; they tend to appear in library journals and *Quill & Quire*.

Of 77: *Best Canadian Stories* the Ontario School Library Association said:

". . . the stories will have little appeal to the average high school student".

Of *General Ludd*, Barbara Campbell writing in the organ of the Canadian book trade, *Quill & Quire*, said:

". . . Metcalf's humour is at time superb. However, it is coloured by ferocious cynicism, suggesting a distorted vision that almost destroys credibility. This is unfortunate, since the central figure, Jim Wells, who is obsessed with restoring a respect for literature, clarifies some serious problems in Canadian publishing."

Petulant Reviews

The following review of *Second Impressions* by Judith Fitzgerald appeared in *Quill & Quire* (Sept. 1981), a paper very important to writers because it is widely used by librarians who are guided by its reviews in their purchases.

"Perhaps because I was so impressed with the excellence of *First Impressions* (Oberon), I had been inadvertently set up for a disappointment, especially since the 1980 trilogy contained a fine introduction and high quality prose by such writers as Martin Avery. This second volume is second rate, not because of its writers, but because for John Metcalf, *Second Impressions* is indeed just that. So content with what he had written in his introduction the first time around, Metcalf felt compelled to recycle much of it for this book. It's distressing when editors write from this disengaged stance, content with blowing their own apathetic horns, not even leaving the reader with the small consolation that it's better than nothing.

I came to the writers themselves with relief . . .

[Here follow three brief paragraphs on Peter Behrens, Ernest Hekkanen, and Linda Svendsen.]

The three young authors in *Second Impressions* deserve a

second look; the short story doesn't suffer here, although the writers may, if only because of their second-hand introduction."

The Review Petulant typically concentrates on reviewing dust-jackets or imperfect bindings. When they've got the bit between their teeth, reviewers do *go on* — and often with little regard for veracity. In the Introduction to *Second Impressions* I did indeed repeat matter from the Introduction to *First Impressions* because I needed it as a starting point. The facts are that the Introduction to *Second Impressions* was 234 lines in length of which 14 only were repeated. Because of some mad bee in her bonnet, the reviewer squandered nearly 50% of her review on the "second-hand" introduction thus taking away attention from the writers she professes to admire and further damaging them by limiting library sales of the book in which they appear.

There is little point in protesting against reviews which are factually incorrect; the review in print, the damage is done.

(sic)

Once every couple of years or so a review appears to which the reviewee returns again and again with wonder and awe. Because the following review appeared in a literary publication of limited circulation I make no apologies for quoting at length; it is the kind of literary experience one wishes to share. It was written by Carol Leckner for *Cross Country*. Carol Leckner is a poet, published, inevitably, by Fred Cogswell.

"A writer must understand the perception of the piece they're embarking on, work from inside its vision and get inside the characters, all this even before starting to get it down. It involves power, and the power to write issues out from within the writer like the current moves the water of the stream. Without the current, there is no stream, and the stream is life itself to all that comes in contact with it. If it moves clear and right, the flow is ongoing and nourishing; if it does not, it still may be attractive but in time, will overflow, become dry or stagnant. The loss of its power will also be the loss of its own life.

So it is with writing. Where the writer does not flow clear and right with the current of their vision, there will be a limited craft. Writing, like all art, lives in the fullness of itself, exploring all the levels it lives in and all the arteries of character and situation. If some levels, or arteries, are left untouched by the inner vision, or by the perspective of the piece, the creation begins to break apart, like a bridge robbed of its pivotal pieces: the link between writer and audience will be unsure and will live only as a part of its whole self.

It is against these criteria that the stories in John Metcalf's *Teeth of My Father* lay motionless. The beautifully textured phrases of description capture habits, physical movements, mantelpieces, a meticulousness of 'particular life', as one of his characters calls it. Metcalf, too, 'manoeuvres' what people do, situations they pass through, but I sense him in the old man speaking of the craft of writing:

'All else is tricks of the trade or inexpressible.'

Perhaps the biggest disappointment was 'Beryl', a story of a university student working at the Leicester Coop Bakery who is attracted to Beryl, a provocative 17-18-year-old whom he 'stares across at as openly as he dares'. Oh, the build-up of the budding romance, ripening with every movie attended, gin and tonic sipped, please and thank you's of his gentle heart, and soul wishing and waiting. But right in the middle, as you yourself are receiving the story and stroking all its fine and tender parts, Metcalf finds the ending and imposes it. The young man is apologizing for not being able to (a bed-ridden grandmother in the next room and a full bladder prompt him to lie about an 'operation'), and I call for surgery! Re-open the story! Its life stream was interrupted, full flow, rounding a curve in its path. Why, when Metcalf was beginning to get to the inexpressible (that artists and sages are meant to make manifest), did he let it go? Unless he considers himself a superficial writer, part of his duty is not to fence-sit, but to dwell within the inexpressible and relay the knowledge received therefrom. It's a precarious position, but a necessary one. Otherwise, he is a Sunday writer, pulling words in from the waves and exhibiting them on appliquéd mantelpieces, a strange taxidermy, when the story lived and he should have been right in there with it, writing from within the power of his vision and the truth of the life of the story.

And he seems to vacillate in opinion about writing and writers in the personae of his characters; whether they are intellectuals, snobs, plain Joes, etc. Why the questioning? Just be it! Create the characters and let them live fully! Without that freedom, they, and the stories, stand like ghosts on an empty sea, waving in the air for life. Give them that life, their full expression."

Comstockery

These kinds of reviews are not as frequent now as they were ten years ago but will doubtless crop up in the future as more and more people are born-again. I was cited as a smut-hound and spoiler of youth a few years ago in a pamphlet circulated to school boards across the country which listed lewd books and quoted undesirable snatches; had the smut been my smut, I'd have been overjoyed but the compilers managed to confuse me with Mordecai Richler.

Like Evelyn Waugh, I keep a sharp eye on this kind of enthusiasm because with luck and a good lawyer it might provide a delightful windfall.

"Once shed of a sort of sophomoric wit, not to mention a fixation with gutter expletives, the author should be able to produce fiction of a challenging character."

(David M. Legate. Montreal *Star*. 1972)

"Why would he spoil an otherwise very funny book by writing in the poorest of poor taste. It can't be the excuse many so-called authors have, that they can't write. Metcalf has proven otherwise . . . . In *Going Down Slow* the really fine humour, the excellent writing, the skills of a craftsman, is unfortunately lost in childish four-letter words which instead of producing shock, merely induces disgust.

It is a pity the fine writing, sharply depicted scenes and finely drawn satire has been smirched by unnecessary filth."

(Ted Burgoyne. Victoria *Daily Colonist*. 1972)

It should not be necessary to draw attention to the grammatical confusions of this second quotation. One wonders what it is that newspaper editors *do* to earn their keep.

Literary Theory

Some reviews either express or reveal fragments of strange literary theories which underlie the reviewer's critical position. Such glimpses into the reviewer's mind can be sobering. Some of these reviews are difficult to understand; the reviewer's critical underpinnings are like a figure in thick fog which is sensed rather than seen. Others are all too clear.

"*Girl in Gingham* contains two short novels . . . . The first 'Private Parts', is subtitled 'A Memoir'. As such, it recounts the narrator's early life in England. Since Metcalf was born and lived his formative years in Britain, it is safe to assume the narrator is the author."

(Michael O. Nowlan. *The Oromocto Post.* 1978)

"Everything possible has been done to make *Going Down Slow* seem like it doesn't have a plot — as I suppose is the fashion in fiction these days."

(Eugene Chadbourne. *Herald Magazine.* 1972)

"Since I had never read anything of John Metcalf's before, I didn't enter the novel with any preconceived notions of his style, subject matter or any of that other rather boring stuff. And I liked what I read."

(Alan Mouse. *The Vanguard.* Yarmouth, Nova Scotia.)

"Its contents may be paralleled with that of a lyric poem, the pleasure is in the reading, not in the depth of experience or meaning . . . . I got the feeling through a reading of 'The Lady Who Sold Furniture', that Metcalf has mastered the technical side of writing, and that it is just a matter of time before he arrived with the right subject matter for the novel."

(Eldon Garnet. Toronto *Telegram.* 1970)

"One senses in this collection that Metcalf is at a watershed in his writing career. So far, he has been recording bits and pieces of experience but has yet to extract any really significant and integrated meaning from these experiences . . . . It is time for him to become a writer, in the largest sense of the word, and an artist."

(Brian Vintcent. *Quill & Quire*. 1975)

"The reality upon which he draws is undoctored."

(Jill Storey. Hamilton *Spectator*. 1978)

"In 'Private Parts' Metcalf also shows an annoying tendency to build to a climax, then leave the reader, well, dangling. When, for example, the teenaged narrator (*sic*) drunkenly vomits into his friend's father's hi-fi — which they'd specially been forbidden to use — the story skips on to a new section without ever telling us what happened next."

(Michael Smith. *Books in Canada*. 1978)

"Both are written in Metcalf's usual style of connected narrative, and both are a blend of the comic and the pathetic . . . . Indeed, 'Private Parts: A Memoir' uses the techniques of Jewish humour to explore the sexual difficulties of a Gentile world."

(Roderick Harvey. *Canadian Literature*. 1980)

Well! What a spavined collection of old war-horses! Lyric poems not "meaning" anything, the story as mere rehearsal for the novel, the demands for "philosophical" statements, Michael Smith, Editor of *Books in Canada*, pretending not to understand, or not understanding, that narratives can move forward in images . . .

Oh, God!

Let my people go!

In some ways, I suppose, it's all uneasily comic and should simply be ignored. And yet. As Mordecai Richler is fond of saying. And yet. The author of the first plonking quotation, Michael O. Nowlan, is not some backwoods chaw-bacon but a high school teacher who — O Canada! — was responsible for designing the programme of CanLit studies for the entire province of New Brunswick.

Sometimes these reviews arrive through my letter-box on a bleak morning when the marmalade has run out or the damn kids have scoffed all the Rice Krispies before I got up and then, weakened by a sense of the world's injustice, I give in to the urge to reply.

Such was the case with the following review by Joan Hind-Smith in *Quill & Quire*.

"Now that Oberon Press has completed its eighth annual collection of short stories, it ought to reconsider the virtue of simply providing a *mélange* of good work. This book, like its predecessors, combines established and new writers, but each story is so charged with individuality that, taken together, they tend to cancel each other out.

[Here the reviewer writes of individual stories.]

In 1971 when Oberon Press began publishing this series, the mere presence of such a book was a miracle. This is no longer the case. Since then there have been collections with sharper focus. Doubleday's *Aurora* edited by Morris Wolfe clearly had the advantage of the guiding mind of one strong editor. While the editors of the current Oberon offering, John Metcalf and Clark Blaise, know a good story when they see one, they include too many points of view. The time has come for Oberon to select."

Enraged by lack of marmalade, I brooded over this singular exhibition of critical insight. It was difficult to know where to start. I had rarely seen a review so starkly potty. Who the hell was this Joan Hind-Smith? On internal textual evidence, possibly a doxy of Morris Wolfe's. I allowed myself a few playful flourishes with the possibilities in 'Hindquarters' and other anus-related epithets and then, breathing deeply, took pen in hand to continue the task of education.

"Joan Hind-Smith's review of *78: Best Canadian Stories* in the January issue of *Quill & Quire* was a sorry effort. In her opening paragraph she says, 'Oberon Press . . . ought to reconsider the virtue of simply providing a *mélange* of good work.' Why should Oberon Press reconsider? Because 'each story is so charged with individuality that, taken together, they tend to cancel each other out.'

With what, then, would Joan Hind-Smith replace 'a *mélange* of good work'? She doesn't actually say but a clue seems to be offered when she talks of collections with a 'sharper focus'. She mentions Morris Wolfe's editing of *Aurora* — 'the guiding mind of one strong editor'. She then implies that the combined minds of Clark Blaise and myself are in sum less strong than the mind of Morris Wolfe. (This may well be so. I've never met Morris Wolfe so I've no idea. But if we do meet, I shall certainly approach him with marked diffidence.)

What she actually means by 'sharper focus' when speaking of *Aurora*, if she means anything at all, is beyond me. Morris Wolfe in the opening paragraph of his introduction states that the purpose of *Aurora* is to provide 'an annual showcase for the best previously unpublished work we can find on whatever subject, in whatever form', a focus which suggests the shotgun rather than the telescopic sight.

Hind-Smith smoothes our ruffled feathers by admitting that 'they know a good story when they see one' but then continues 'they include too many points of view. The time has come for Oberon to select'. Can it be that she wants stories *less* individual and all about the same sort of thing? *The Oberon Book of Canadian Marital Discord Stories 1979? 1980: Best Canadian Domestic Pet Stories?*

Whatever it may be that the lady wants, she ought to learn that there's really no *point* in criticizing an apartment block for not being a town house. When an anthology selected on the stated basis of quality is criticized for 'individuality' and for including 'too many points of view', I think the time has come not for Oberon to select but for the selection by *Quill & Quire* of a reviewer less obviously perverse."

I *should* have addressed myself, of course, to the point that stories, unless they're *very* bad, don't have "points of view" but it would have been a waste of good pearls. This struggle against sub-literary critics is not rewarding; the supply is inexhaustible.

Presumptuous Reviews

These reviews presume personal knowledge of the author and are usually tinged by an inexplicable irritation or hostility.

"Metcalf is refreshingly uninhibited about lampooning Canada's 'ethnics'. Maybe he has imported a kind of spiritual Paki-bashing from his homeland ... Susan is Lebanese; her parents are figures of fun to David for that reason."
                    (Kildare Dobbs. Toronto *Daily Star*. 1972)

An uncharacteristically sloppy review by Dobbs. Susan's parents in *Going Down Slow* are not figures of fun because they are Lebanese but because they are extremely *weird* Lebanese. In several reviews of *Going Down Slow* it was assumed that because I drew a portrait of one Gagnon, an unappetizing janitor, I was making some sort of comment on French Canadians in general. This kind of assumption baffles me.

I was not unprepared for accusations of anti-semitism over my novel *General Ludd* but only Cary Fagan in a remarkably silly review in *The Canadian Forum* came close to the suggestion.

The following review from *Maclean's* is a small miracle of dishonesty and deranged nationalism — doubtless an expression of the zeal of the convert.

"In these alienated times what a novelist needs is not roots, but withered roots .... The book's main flaw is Metcalf's alienation from the New World. He complains, for instance, about the barbaric spelling of Canadian Tire. Readers who don't know rugger songs are simply lacking in culture. Metcalf's roots, however authentically withered, are on the wrong side of the Atlantic."
                    (John Muggeridge. *Maclean's*. 1978)

This extract is from a review of *Girl in Gingham*. The reference to the spelling of 'Tire' is to page 19 of *Going Down Slow*. It's an *unusual* procedure to attack a book by attributing to it some of the content of an entirely different book.

I, of course, do not complain about the spelling of 'Tire'; David does.

(Another outbreak of the Michael Smiths.)

There is not one word in *Girl in Gingham* or *Going Down Slow* to suggest that author or narrator knows or likes 'rugger songs';

there is nothing in either book to suggest that author or narrator would equate 'rugger songs' with culture.

John Muggeridge, apparently the son of Malcolm Muggeridge, is not just some mindless yo-yo but is a teacher at college level. He concludes by suggesting that if a writer wasn't born in Canada, he shouldn't write in Canada. Or possibly he's attempting to say that writing about a country other than Canada isn't, or shouldn't be, of interest to Canadians.

I'm left wondering about the exact nature of his problems.

It's a pity that such a *very* naughty review was approved and printed by the most widely circulated magazine in the country. But it's not surprising.

"Since Wells (Jim Wells in *General Ludd*) devotes all his energy to speeches about the decline of the West, the plot is allowed to wander by itself into various strange corners. For no particular reason we visit Wells' country place, six useless acres and an old stone farmhouse which may or may not be modelled on a stone house in Delta, Ont., home of author John Metcalf .... He (Metcalf) now produces his own fiction, collects grants, and writes-in-residence at universities."

(Don Stanley. Vancouver *Province*. 1980)

This review may or may not have been prompted by envy.

These presumptuous reviews do, I must admit, feed my latent paranoia. They'd feed anyone's. I was left uneasy by a recent review in the Ottawa *Citizen*. It was a generous and positive review by Patricia Morley of *81: Best Canadian Stories*. It contained no personal references to me whatsoever. It nowhere employed the word 'painful' or 'dated'. In one corner of the review appeared a photograph of me taken some five years ago by a *Citizen* reporter.

The attack was non-linear — if not surrealistic.

Under the photograph, in italic, were the words:
Less 'painful' — or is he dated?

The inverted commas seemed to imply quotation though, given the *Citizen*, not necessarily so. I read the review again to make sure.

Nothing.

The waitress in the cafe where I go in the morning for coffee said,
"Saw your picture in the paper. What didja do?"
I'm still wondering.

Semi-Literate Reviews

All the types of review I've so far illustrated are unimportant compared with this last and largest category. It would be excessively tedious to illustrate this type fully; there have been depressing samples already given under different headings. Let us just say that it is the most common.

Consider the following:

"Private Parts the best of 2 stories"
                (Headline in the Hamilton *Spectator*. 1978)

From a very favourable review of *81: Best Canadian Stories*:

"This anthology contains some stories by better-known Canadian authors, such as Mavis Gallant and Alice Munro, and some by writers who deserve more notoriety."
                                        (Calgary *Herald*. 1981)

"Wickedly satirical, brilliantly written, continuously entertaining, this account of a poet at odds with almost everything in a Department of Creative Writing is more than an attack upon false attitudes and values. It is something of an inditement of our whole culture and, in its radical clarity, reminds one of both Orwell and Swift, though the style has a fast-paced zest that is all Metcalf's own."
                                        (*The Malahat Review*. 1981)

The word they intended was 'indictment'; there's a difference.
But enough.
This is not fun.
Enough.

I hope that it has become obvious by now that this essay is not an extended settling of petty scores, that I am not concerned with a purely *personal* bunch of sour grapes. The reviews from which I've quoted have been drawn from newspapers and journals from Nova Scotia to British Columbia. Some of the reviews have been taken from small provincial papers, others from the largest and most powerful papers in the country. The whole point of this essay is that the dreary story these reviews spell out *is a story that could have been told by any writer in this country.*

The only paper in Canada with *consistently* respectable book pages is the Toronto *Globe and Mail* and the most consistent and dependable newspaper critic in the country is the *Globe*'s William French. But one man on one newspaper is not enough.

Reviewing in Canada is badly paid and is usually carried on by amateurs. The two facts are not unrelated. Reviewing is badly paid because most newspapers are not prepared to disburse even a small part of their large profits on a section of the paper which is of interest to only 1% of the readership. This percentage reflects the importance we place on literature and the arts in general. That the educated middle class acquiesces in this sound business decision reflects the general *irrelevance* of the arts in Canada.

Far too much reviewing is done by writers. Writers can be got cheap. The Canadian literary world is small and there are few writers sufficiently magisterial to deliver totally disinterested opinion; puffery and pulled punches are inevitable when the reviewer knows that next week he must meet the author in a social or professional context. We have no V. S. Pritchetts or Anthony Burgesses nor do we have magazines which would carry reviews of the kind they write. We do not have such magazines because there are not enough people in Canada to support them.

It is obvious that we need more literary journalists. We need magazines and newspapers which will pay them well for their work. But it is equally obvious that we're not going to get such work unless there is a demand for it, unless, in other words, there is an audience. And despite the pronouncements of the Secretary of State, the activities of the Canada Council,

Discovery Trains, and Hug-A-Canadian-Author-Week, it seems to me that the Emperor remains bollock naked.

But let us not, as Evelyn Waugh used to write, repine.

Whatever the dreary realities, it is vital that we live in faith.

I am neither a fusspot nor a pedagogue. I hope I have not given the impression in this essay that I have been merely *niggling*. I am stalking a far larger quarry. It is my quaint contention that writing is a moral act. I believe that literature is one of the most important expressions of our imaginative, moral, and national life. The reception and discussion of that literature by readers and critics is therefore of fundamental importance.

As "communication" increases, literacy declines. When language is slighted and abused, wounds are inflicted on our social body. As our ability to use language degenerates, we become increasingly impoverished — socially, intellectually, artistically, and morally. As concision, grace, concinnity, and elegance decline, the country grows shapeless and barbaric.

If we would achieve greatness, we must mind our P's and Q's.

We Are Honoured This Evening

STRANGE BUSINESS, READINGS. Paid for by The Canada Council, of course, or else there wouldn't be any. They're not really worth it for me anymore unless they're local or the going is getting rough. $125.00 plus travel expenses, which usually works out to three days of lost work for about $41.00 per day. Day getting there, day getting back, day recovering while the mind clears itself of flying, drinking, talking, and smiling.

It's always the same. Met at the airport and driven to the hotel suffering from Air Canada chicken. In the hotel you can't turn the heat in your room below 100° and there are water-colours on the wall of Peggy's Cove. Introduced to all the Canlit noddies, dinner in some foul restaurant where the menu's French but the food isn't. The reading. The entertainment of questions. The reception. Driven back to the hotel by somebody who feels compelled to point out all the local landmarks which you can't see even if you wanted to because it's dark.

A lousy night's sleep because of the festive conventioneers who are vomiting in the corridors and knocking on your door and then saying sorry they were looking for good old Mabel.

And then back to the everywhere identical airport where you board, drink too much, eat the chicken and the potatoes sculpted into small balls and read *Sports Illustrated* because the buggers up front got the newspapers and the two copies of *Time*.

This passage from *General Ludd* is, of course, fiction.

Reality is unbelievably more curious and entertaining.

It's always rather puzzled me what people get out of public readings. I can understand what writers get out of them; they get $150.00. Those writers adjudged "senior" by The Canada Council are allowed to do twelve readings per year and the $1,800.00 (less tax) they can earn in this way is an important chunk of a writer's income as there are few writers in Canada who earn more than $10,000 from their literary activities. But what do readers get?

If the writers are skilled as performers, the audience enjoys something theatrical but few writers possess such skills. Leon Rooke always turns in bravura performances and John Newlove on his good nights exercises an almost hypnotic rhetoric but, in the main, public readings are slim pickings.

There's a legitimate interest in hearing a poet read because the voice sometimes indicates meanings and nuances which had eluded the eye. We're conditioned to the printed page and I've often protested myself that readers don't seem to *hear*. Readings are perhaps valuable in that they recall readers to the central importance of *voice* but I'm not convinced that this is what audiences get out of them.

If audiences are not there to be amused and entertained — and surely only someone with a pretty spartan sense of fun could be genuinely entertained by most poetry readings — and if they're not there as knowledgeable readers seeking to deepen their appreciation of work already familiar to them, why *do* they muster?

The composition of audiences is a puzzle. At universities they're made up of members of the English department doing their duty and dragooned CanLit students. At more public venues, it's been my experience that 50% or more of the audience has never read anything by the writer and that approximately a quarter of the audience *has never heard of the writer*. I'm not trying to bite the hand of the 50% that feeds but I must admit that the *other* 50% per cent disturbs me.

There's a hard core of very *strange* people who are attracted to artistic and cultural events for reasons unknown, people who write in the dark with flashlights attached to their pens, people who *hum*, people who laugh immoderately in the wrong place, people who buttonhole the reader afterwards and relate details of unappetizing works-in-progress. And nearly always there is one in the audience who afterwards says, "I wonder if you know the name of a nature book I once read. I've forgotten the author and the title but it was very interesting. It was about otters."

It would not be accurate to describe these people as "groupies" because quite a few of them tend to be actively hostile or contemptuous. Here is a sketch of a type.

The reader is chatting with a small group of people afterwards. A young man stands on the fringe of the group. He is pallid and oddly tense. He is waiting. At last he moves closer. He does not say hello or remark on the reading; such pleasantries are beneath him; he has urgencies he will not sully with small-talk.

"I wanted to ask you", he says.

The reader puts on a face of pleased enquiry.

"What is your opinion of Doris Lessing?"

"Well", says the reader, starting to babble, "she's a bit too *intelligent* for my taste, if you know what I mean. I mean, *ideas* are paramount, that *as fiction* — well, someone who strikes me in exactly the same sort of way is Colin Wilson if you've . . . though of course Wilson is much *loonier* than Lessing but . . ."

"That", interrupts the young man, "is precisely what I would have expected you to say."

He stalks off.

And returns to some grim basement apartment where, justified and resolute, he takes up work at page 724 of a novel-in-progress, a work with Nietzschean underpinnings, a work which makes no concessions.

At nearly every reading I've done, people have come up to me at the end and said, *I don't mind admitting that I've never read any of your books, but after tonight, by golly, I'm going to go and . . .*

The sales of my work have remained at a fairly constant figure over the years so I've been led to believe that these hundreds of 'converts' are either dedicated library-users or sadists.

Many people go to readings, I suspect, simply to see someone of whom they've heard — though that *still* doesn't explain the people who go to see someone of whom they've *never* heard. I can understand and share the desire to see the famous though 'famous' in the case of Canadian writers is pitching it a little strong. Years ago, I went to hear W. H. Auden read at McGill University simply because I wanted to see that amazing *face*. I learned nothing from his reading that I hadn't heard before but I enjoyed his slippers, his haystack of manuscript, his tattered books, and his shirt hanging out of his trousers. I happened to be sitting next to George Bowering who made some condescending remark about how curious it was in this day and age to hear stuff actually written in pentameters, a remark that, nearly fifteen years later, still makes me wish I had leaned across and stuck my finger up his nose.

Most poetry readings, however, make me slightly crazy with boredom and suppressed rage. I attend readings given by other people only from a sense of duty and solidarity. I'd far rather read their work at my own pace and in private peace. The *churchy* feel of these events depresses me. I'm all for culture but Culture makes me squirm.

The most gruelling poetry reading I ever endured was one delivered by Jay Macpherson in 1975. I attended only because it was sponsored by the seat of learning at which I was employed. I went in fairly grim mood because Jay Macpherson's verse is a bit twee and attenuated for my taste and also because I was half-way through a new Travis McGhee which bulged with well-described violence. My wife accompanied me. She was lured forth only by the promise of dinner afterwards; she is not a lover of poetry and had doubtless been planning on laying hands on Travis in my absence. We took our seats feeling hollow and looking forward to the dinner that would be ours in about one hour.

Jay Macpherson had just published a new book after eighteen years or so of writer's block. She explained the conception and gestation of her new poems, something, as I recall, to do with a horror film she'd chanced to see. She then read these poems. My wife was making soft moaning noises. Jay Macpherson then explained the genesis of a related sequence of poems in the collection which were about a teddy bear. The teddy bear was sometimes called Ted and sometimes Tedwold. And to make matters even more appalling, the poems were, in a maidenly sort of way, confessional.

My wife started punching my thigh.

I stared ahead impassively.

Gradually, it became obvious that it was Jay Macpherson's intention to read *the whole bloody book*. Poem followed poem, page after page.

My wife whispered viciously, "You *putz!* You rotten putz!"

By the time the lugubrious doings of Tedwold drew to a close, most decent restaurants other than Chinese had closed their doors. My wife's eyes were bright with unshed tears of rage. After a wild cab ride, we managed to squeak into *Chez Ma Mère*

Michelle, credit-carding our way through food we couldn't afford and drinking excessively in hysterical silence.

Most Canadian poetry is desperately bad but the same is true of most poetry in England and the United States. I recently renewed my subscription to the Poetry Book Society in England and received what their panel of experts considered the four best books of poetry published in England in that year; all were trivial and posturing.

I'm slightly ashamed to admit that I've lost touch with most contemporary American poetry. For a time I kept up with Roethke, Stanley Kunitz, Donald Justice, Robert Creeley, Galway Kinnell, Robert Bly, Larry Rubin, Robert Hayden, Donald Hall, and W. S. Merwin but my interest began to drift in the mid-seventies. I realized that I admired John Crowe Ransom above any of them. The only contemporary British poet who affords keen pleasure is Philip Larkin but in his last book there was a falling away from earlier work. Seamus Heaney's first book, *Death of a Naturalist*, was exciting but — heretical opinion — succeeding books have seemed to me muddied.

I've thought for a long time that the very act now of "writing a poem" is so artificial that it places the poet in a hopelessly self-conscious position before he even starts. Poems written without form and in the language of *very* ordinary men are no answer to this sense of irrelevance; they're rather too much like reading an underground newspaper and in most instances are written with about as much skill. Poems characterized by relaxation and unconventional orthography such as those written by George Bowering and other adherents of the Ampersand School seem unlikely to revitalize a prostrate art. I've sometimes thought that poetry might regain vitality by deliberately returning to obvious artifice but possibly it's too late for any form of resuscitation. I'm profoundly sad that this is so and acutely aware that short stories will be the next genre to succumb.

One of the reasons for poetry's decline — and for the decline of all serious literature — is that society treats its children differently from the way we were treated and children, in turn, have quite different attitudes to adult society. Adults now make far less effort to hand on to their children their patrimony and children are now less eager to become adults. When my wife was a child, she refused to read books with illustrations in them because she considered such books "babyish"; our own children ask us, "Will I be able to understand it?"

Thirty or forty years ago, there was a continuity and community between adults and children which has now been severely shaken. The classic children's books — such books as *Treasure Island* and *The Wind in the Willows*, for example — are books that can be read with pleasure by adults. Since my childhood there has grown up a genre which caters to young teenagers and which speaks directly to their separate world; these books are typically concerned with "problems": race-relations, divorce, peer-pressures, sexuality, justice, etc. In other words, they address "ideas" and so, with their sociological and psychological motivations, undermine the possibilities of *literary* response. Although many of these books wear the trappings of *The Catcher in the Rye*, they are stamped, covertly, with the Good Housekeeping Seal of Approval. I can see myself, child on knee, as it were, reading aloud the wondrous doings of Toad of Toad's Hall but I'm damned if I'm going to read aloud how Jennifer's Thoughtless Mother didn't adequately prepare her for womanhood and how during Language Arts a Spreading Stain . . .

A few weeks ago, I was buying some paperbacks for my younger children and came across a work whose blurb claimed that the story would be useful in teaching children "the acceptability of expressing anger".

Mermaids was what I was after.

Vast and indefinable commercial pressures exist to exploit children and teenagers and these pressures are dedicated to inventing and propagating a distinct and separate pre-adult world; this world is hostile to taste and intelligence and is inevitably hostile to the past. The commercial world celebrates fashion, technology, and change itself. Poetry cannot compete against the volume-control on the TV or stereo and is defenceless against the gobbling attacks of Pac Man. We once exploited and corrupted "natives" with trade beads; we now use their equivalents to exploit and corrupt our own children.

Recently, in search of diversion, I insinuated myself into a press conference arranged for Jean-Jacques Blais, the Minister in charge of the 1981 Canadian census. He thanked the Canadian public for their support of this undertaking — not mentioning, of course, that lack of "support" would have

203

resulted in severe punishment. He went on to say how useful the demographic and sociological data would be to Industry. What he *meant* was that these figures would make it easier for hucksters to identify and manipulate markets. And "markets" means you and me and, more defencelessly, our children.

I have a lively sense that everything I value has been driven to the wall by what are called "commercial interests", by hucksters with degrees in Business Administration from our seats of learning who hustle breakfast cereal and scratch-and-smell books.

And what has all this rant to do with the decline of poetry?

Everything.

I look upon the world I inhabit with considerable distaste and gloom; I'm beginning to suspect that I may end my days in a loony bin after an unprovoked and murderous assault on a McDonald's hostess.

The present situation of poetry in our society might be suggested by eisteddfods, lugubrious cultural "revivals" featuring a lot of fervent Welshmen clad in bedsheets declaiming incomprehensible poems written in complex medieval forms, the whole extravanganza reverentially broadcast by BBC-TV as an annual penitential offering.

Natural material, one would have thought, for Benny Hill.

(Prose has its own poetry, of course, and I've always tried to champion that poetry and do the dirty to its enemy "prose poetry"; such books as Elizabeth Smart's *By Grand Central Station I Sat Down and Wept* fill me with loathing. How masterful and genuinely poetic are such lines as these:

> In the late summer of that year we lived in a house in a village that looked across the river and the plain to the mountains. In the bed of the river there were pebbles and boulders, dry and white in the sun, and the water was clear and swiftly moving and blue in the channels.

I'm a bit hesitant about "and blue in the channels" but it's surely impossible to deny the magic and grandeur of this writing.)

But if the poetry itself tends to be drab, some aspect or another of public readings can always be relied upon to provide entertainment. I once attended a reading given by Al Purdy prior to which we'd entertained him generously at dinner. By the time he reached the podium he was three sheets in the wind and alarmingly pale. He began to introduce the first poem he was going to read, seeming a bit vague about the matter, and then stopped mid-sentence. He groped in his jacket and brought out a packet of cigarettes — an unusual departure from his plastic-tipped cigars. He extracted a cigarette and set it between his lips with the filter-tip pointing outwards. As he took out a book of matches, I've rarely seen an audience so rivetted.

In high schools, readings are inevitably enlivened by the p.a. system ordering a list of 37 students to report to the school nurse or by the school band in an adjacent room breaking into *America the Beautiful*.

At a recent reading by John Newlove, a rat appeared and toured the auditorium, doubtless confirming and strengthening John's view of the nature of things.

My own readings are always, for me at least, enjoyable. I enjoy jetting about Canada at someone else's expense and I enjoy being taken out to dinner and I enjoy the gossip at the dinner table as alcohol loosens tongues and one is regaled with the *true* details of what Margaret Atwood did last time she was there. And then there's the catching up to do on faculty infidelities. All very enjoyable.

Some of these dinners, however, have turned out to be somewhat awkward. On one occasion, in an effort to be entertaining, I launched into a performance on the subject of F. P. Grove only to discover that one of my hosts had published learned articles on the old duffer and considered him the next best thing to white sliced. I felt a bit like Bertie Wooster telling Esmond Haddock's deaf aunt the one about the deaf man in the railway carriage, the saga of which can be found in *The Mating Season*.

On another occasion, I found myself dining with a man who the week before had published a review of my most recent story collection opining that it was pinchbeck and tedious. Oddly enough, this was exactly the opinion *I* held of *his* poetry. But dinner was so surprisingly good that I soon gave up the idea of doing him a sudden mischief.

The necessary small-talk on these occasions can sometimes be uphill work. If guest and host are not hitting it off, one or the other in an access of embarrassment will seize upon some proffered topic and talk with insane desperation. I once lectured an authority on Henry James about T. J. Wise's forgeries — a subject about which I know very little. John Newlove once told me that on one such uncomfortable evening he'd found himself arguing passionately and at tedious length that Walter de la Mare was the most important poet of the twentieth century. He was as amazed as his dinner companions but couldn't stop.

After the dinner, one is escorted to the hall one is to play where one's host apologizes for the size of the audience very decently attributing it to the inclement weather or the fact that exams are just starting or finishing or the presence that evening on campus of a major rock group. The host also out of decency and in self-justification details the number of posters he had had printed and apologizes for the fact that the local newspaper omitted to print an announcement, the reason for which he really can't understand because they're usually very good about that sort of thing . . .

. . . oh, and the man from Technical Services hasn't shown up so unfortunately the microphone system or whatever you call it . . .

These rituals over, the introducer plays *his* part.

This part of the ritual is always entertaining because the introducer has usually acquired his knowledge of the guest, hurriedly, from imperfect sources and often manages astounding cock-ups by misquoting titles or attributing to the reader works he has not written. Over the years, I've had some pretty strange stuff attributed to me. The title that always causes trouble is *Sixteen by Twelve* which has been announced in amazing permutations. I know that it sounds like the wilder reaches of invention, but it is sober truth that one introducer, a chief librarian, attributed to me a collection of short stories entitled *McGraw-Hill*.

(These misunderstandings remind me of a reading given by P. K. Page. It must have been a long time ago because she had recently published *Cry Ararat!*. I had enjoyed the collection and after the reading asked her if she'd mind signing my copy. We chatted for a few minutes and she made some comments about my own writing which were obviously intended as compliments but whose exact meaning and application were obscure. She obviously *liked* my stuff but seemed to have a very *personal* view of what I was trying to do. All became clear, however, when I got home and glanced inside the book; the inscription read: *For John Newlove . . .*)

After the reading come the questions. The room is soggy with silent embarrassment. A member of the audience, compelled by duty and decency, asks something and the reader seizes upon this question and talks and talks, driving the audience *and* himself close to the verge as all everyone presumably wants is to get at the cash-bar or gallon jugs of Algerian red. I *hate* questions and now instruct introducers that I'm most unwilling to entertain them. One doesn't question the cast of a play or interrogate jugglers and readers-in-public *ought* to have elevated themselves to the same category.

Questions delay the curtain, fritter away emotional impact. Readings should be performances.

One Canadian writer who is *never* embarrassed in such situations is Hugh Hood. Hugh *likes* questions and gives each one, however daft, his fullest consideration. A typical Hoodian reply will tend to refer to Dante, Spenser, Wordsworth, Coleridge, Haydn, Mozart, Proust, Anthony Powell, P. G. Wodehouse and, with stern distaste, Emily Carr, all of whose colours Hugh finds depressing and all of whose shapes he claims to be vulval. During the length of the reply, sidetrips will have been essayed to the influence of Methodism on nineteenth-century publishing and the banking practices of the Holy Roman Empire. Every one of Hugh's answers might be described as a *lazzo*.

A question which *always* comes up if students are in the audience is some variant of: Are all those meanings/symbols/metaphors/images *really* in your story or . . . ? One probably has to have been a teacher to work out what is behind this question. It reflects the running battle between teacher and students. The student is hoping that the reader will say that the painstaking analysis of stories by the teacher is a lot of deluded nonsense; the question reflects the fact that the students simply are not persuaded by all this imagery compulsion from which their instructors suffer. Most students seem to feel strongly that we murder to dissect. I always come down on the side of the teacher but not without misgivings. Far too many teachers *do* suffer from a severe case of the Jack Horners but their unimaginative intellectuality is probably preferable to the unpruned horror of the student mind.

Many people have said that I am somewhat harsh on the subject of the student mind but I know what I know. Many years ago I was one of the examiners for high school matriculation in Quebec. I have read thousands of responses to "sight poems". I cannot forget one year a simple poem descriptive of a skier launching himself down a slope; 35% of Quebec's matriculants stated that the subject matter of the poem concerned a trip by aeroplane.

And since then things have got worse.

Recently, I read to an Adult Creative Writing Class at a community college, invariably the very worst of audiences because they have no interest whatsoever in writing other than their own. I read a relatively new story called "The Eastmill Reception Centre". I read powerfully and with great command of the material. It was, if I say so myself, a splendid perform-ance. When I'd finished, the room was silent.

The click of knitting needles was audible.

The introducer called for questions.

The silence was deafening.

"Well . . .", said the introducer.

And then a hand went up.

A young woman in caftan and clogs.

"Yes?"

"Is that sweater", she said, "hand-knitted?"

After the reading and questions there is usually a reception. These are of three types: a reception within the institution with free wine or a cash-bar, an informal decamping to some nearby tavern for a general booze-up, or a reception at the home of a member of the faculty. This last type tends to be most interest-ing. What happens at these home receptions depends on the personalities of hosts and guests. They are sometimes decorous and end early. More typically, they become drunken and last until the small hours when the invited author trips out onto the silent lawn and shouts:

Oh, morning, at the brown brink eastward, springs —

and then throws up over his hostess' blue spruce.

But before this finale, many things will have happened. The family child will appear in its nightgown and read its book aloud. The family dog, inevitably large and relentlessly friendly, will gobble the paté. An assistant professor will recite *It was my thirtieth year to heaven . . .* and will later be found weeping where the coats are. The wife will glare meaningfully at the husband as he becomes recklessly pissed and will retire in a marked manner leaving to him the aftermath of crackers, curling bread, and drying cheese. The dog will start heaving and will return the paté in roughly its original shape. At about 3:00 a.m. one can usually count on some faculty feud surfacing; bitter, unforgivable words in the brightness of the kitchen.

And then there are ladies.

Decorum prevents my detailing the sexual invitations which are extended with amazing frankness; it's a strange fact and I don't know how to interpret it but all the bedwards invitations I've received have been extended by ladies who drove Volkswagens.

On one of these literary occasions, actually a launching-party for new books by three writers, a well-known Canadian scribbler locked himself in the lavatory where he tried to set fire to the books by his colleagues and competitors.

Most writers, however, settle for slander.

While all of the foregoing is both true *and* typical, I am not unaware of what goes on on the other side of the fence. In 1975 I organized a series of readings at Vanier College in Montreal and I know the problems organizers face: colleagues who wouldn't put in a courtesy appearance for the Second Coming, colleagues who all somehow forget to read to their classes the enticing announcements one has written, students who *en masse* are suddenly faced with grave family crises, the arrogance of college print-shops, department heads who declare sudden bankruptcy, forcing the host to assume personally the financial burden of the sudden craving for larks' tongues which afflicts those eating at an institution's expense.

I'm aware, too, of the host's uneasiness, the surreptitious glances at the wristwatch as the guest becomes increasingly jovial and garrulous and starts addressing the waiter as 'Alfredo'. I know that feeling of impending doom as one realizes that the man one knew last year as a jolly toper has degenerated into a raving dipsomaniac. I can remember that certainty that if the guest downs one more cognac he will lose the faculty of speech.

And then the final embarrassment of addressing the throng of 13:

We are honoured this evening to have with us . . .

I bought in 1956 from the sixpenny tray outside a junk shop a book entitled: *The Readings of Charles Dickens as Arranged and Read by Himself.* The book was published in 1907 but contained an introduction entitled "Charles Dickens as a Reader" by John Hollingshead which had been first published in 1864.

The following quotation from the Introduction describes Dickens at work:

> Mr. Dickens's readings, or illustrations, as we prefer to call them, are running, critical commentaries upon his own works. With all the self-possession, the flexibility of voice, and the facial expression of a trained actor, it is not surprising that Mr. Dickens should be able to cause his own creations to live and move before our eyes. Possessing all the bodily requirements, the conception of character alone is wanted; and there is abundant evidence of the existence of this in the creative fertility of his books. No original dramatic author, no writer of dramatic fiction in the form of novels, whose characters impress their forms upon the page in their own language out of their own mouths, can fail to be in heart, mind, and soul a natural mimic, or actor. Every character in Mr. Dickens's novels, drawn in the first instance from observation, must have been dramatically embodied — acted over, so to speak, a hundred times in the process of development and transference to the written page; and the qualities of voice, nerve, and presence being granted, Mr. Dickens merely passes over that ground, in the face of a large and attentive audience, which he has often passed over before in the undisturbed privacy of his study. Where the pure actor's art is shown, as distinguished from the dramatic quality inherent in all character-cre-

ators, is in certain small alterations of the text of his printed book, so minute as to escape the eye of any but a critical observer, but purposely made to produce effective points. It will be sufficient to name one instance in the "Christmas Carol", where the text seems to be improved in a literary sense by the elision of several words coming after, and destroying, to some extent, the effect of a well-known passage. In the glorious account of the Fezziwig ball, in the printed book Mr. Dickens winds up the description of Mr. Fezziwig's dancing by saying he "cut — cut so deftly, that he appeared to wink with his legs, and came upon his feet again without a stagger". In Mr. Dickens's vocal embodiment, he leaves out all the words that come after "legs" saying, with a spasmodic shake of the head and a twist of the paper knife, "He cut — cut so deftly, that he appeared to — wink with his legs."

Leaving aside the question of whether Dickens' alteration of his text is an improvement — and I think it is — Hollingshead's description raises what are, for me, serious questions about the writer as reader or performer. This account suggests that Dickens was willing to take liberties with his text which I'd be most unwilling to do. I said earlier that readings ought to be performances but perhaps I should qualify what I mean by "performance". I have no reservations about suggesting accents, timbre, or the like and I do believe that the whole performance should be directed to emotional impact but I have stubbornly refused elision or the inclusion of verbal effects not in the text itself because I've always felt that not to refuse them is to insert the thin end of the wedge of improvisation. I feel that the prose *as it stands on the page* should contain all the direction and sugges- tion the reader needs. I insist on my work as prose; I insist on the inclusion of every "he said" and "she said". In other words, something prevents me from turning the formalities of prose into the more immediately engaging arts of the theatre.

The nature of my reservations about theatricality is not very clear even to me but I feel that there's a point where "perform- ance" becomes antagonistic to *literary* values. The theatrical arts are seductive and rather flashy and there's something in my temperament which causes me to accept the flowers, sip the champagne, but keep my legs firmly crossed. I remember listening to a reading by Leo Simpson — a funny story delivered in a charming variety of Irish accents — and I remember asking him afterwards if the story would print. He said he thought it would be far too thin; its pleasures had been largely the pleasures of personality and performance.

David Watmough has built a career and reputation as a writer by reading what are, on the printed page, fairly thin-textured stories. *His* invention, and I admire his colossal nerve, is to call these very ordinary short stories "monodramas". This strikes me as linguistic *chutzpah* of the highest order and it interests me that no one I've talked to finds it as thigh-slappingly funny as I do. The question is: are "monodramas" still "monodramas" when no one's there to hear them?

There are some writers whose work simply wouldn't come across in front of an audience or on radio and that is certainly no criticism of their writing. Henry James springs to mind. But what a pleasure it would have been to have heard Henry James on such a programme as *Twenty Questions!*

I suspect that Robert Weaver's CBC *Anthology* programme and his generous CBC commissions and the annual literary competitions may have had a deleterious effect on the stories produced and on our judgements about writing. A story that "reads" is not necessarily a good story; a story that is "good radio" could well be a story painted in primary colours and bold outlines which would be actively offensive to the private reader. It is much to Bob Weaver's credit that he has never pressured a writer to turn in simplified or popularized work. The very idea would offend him deeply. What concerns me is what writers might have done to themselves.

And perhaps unconsciously.

Many people have told me that they feel my work is very urgent and dramatic and that they've wondered why I haven't attempted writing plays. The answer to that, I suppose, is that I want my work to be totally and absolutely mine; more important, though, I want it to be *formally complete*. I could not tolerate the theatre's necessary sharing of talents. I could not stand the improvisational nature of workshops where the practical demands of the theatre can, quite legitimately, cut lines, paragraphs, and even scenes, changing an action's shape and balance.

People who imagine that it would be a relatively minor matter to change a page of dialogue in a story into stage dialogue probably don't know much about plays and know next to nothing about fiction. A page of well-written dialogue is a thing of great formal beauty; most stage dialogue is not. Prose is complex and demanding; most drama — and that includes film and TV — *must* be simple and uncomplicated. Words, for an actor, are usually the bones which he fleshes out; I'm interested in creating bone, flesh, and spirit in as close to an unalterable form as I can get. Great theatrical performances are ephemeral; great writing is not. If the writing has steely construction, the reader should be affected in much the same way every time he reads it. "Performance" can be the enemy of this ideal of unalterability.

Matadors, according to Hemingway, refer to "brave" bulls as being "on wheels". That is, the "brave" bull always does what it's supposed to; its eyesight is perfect and it charges without quirky deviation in response to every command and suggestion of the cape and muletta. The relationship between book and reader should have the control and inevitability of the *corrida*. The good reader should be "on wheels"; the task of the writer is to make sure that the wheels cannot leave the track, that the reader always hits the cape.

When good actors bend their talents to readings of literary texts, the results *can* be ear-openers. Richard Burton read Dylan Thomas far more effectively than Thomas read Thomas. Jack McGowran's one-man show of selections from Samuel Beckett was not only entrancing but revealed for me previously unheard depths in the text. But these instances are untypical.

Actors, even the best of them, are a rum bunch and are not, in my experience, noted for literary intellect. I would have the gravest reservations about unleashing any of them on something that I had laboured over for endless weeks. The primary loyalty of actors is not to the text; they have their own language and achieve greatness within it. I'm thinking of the language and rhetoric of Buster Keaton, Charlie Chaplin, and Jacques Tati. I was reading recently John Gielgud's autobiography *An Actor and His Time* and was struck by the number of times he quite casually mentioned speeches in various plays whose meanings he never had managed to grasp.

Most public readings, as I've already suggested, are not theatrical triumphs. I really cannot believe that most of them are even mildly entertaining. Nor are they held By Popular Demand as an audience of fifty, even in a large city, is considered heady stuff. Yet every plane that passes overhead is bearing its complement of Canadian writers to some unlikely tryst.

Why?

There are obvious political reasons. Although the money still ends up in the hands of scruffy writers, the idle sods have been required to do something visible to get it; it can be claimed that "the public" has benefited. This is more satisfactory to the bureaucratic and political mind than the still suspect donation of cash to those who, in private, might or might not use it to produce a book. One excellent book will, in the long term, have greater impact and importance than ten thousand readings but excellent books are low on the totem pole for politicians; they prefer *events* — events at which they can be photographed — which goes some way towards explaining why Canada has, proportionately, more ballet companies and theatres than any other country in the Western world.

Our "cultural agencies" are very keen on "democratization". As well they might be. They're in a dodgy position. Questions in the House about aid to layabouts, complaints from taxpayers about nasty sheet-metal sculptures fouling our parks and open spaces, constant bellyaching about the CBC which has in any case bent over backwards to emasculate itself. Any overt expression of anything that could be construed as "elitism" would be to invite the attention of all those Honourable Members whose spiritual home is a Legion Bullhead Supper.

But what is *really* disturbing for unabashed elitists is the suspicion that in our "cultural agencies" there are a few who earnestly and *genuinely* seek the "democratization" of culture. These people frighten me very much. They are usually intellectuals with about as much real grip on the nature of "the people" as my left buttock.

They believe in People's Theatre.

Writers are subsidized, as are magazines, publishers, and printers. The Council even buys its own products which it gives to people who won't buy them. I've sometimes wondered if the growth of The Canada Council Public Readings Programme isn't a covert closing of the subsidy circle, a subtle method of buying the final component, audience.

But I feel that politics is not the whole answer.

Over the last ten years, Public Readings seem to have become an ancient Canadian tradition, a secular rite, a Canadian equivalent of such vestigial activities as the distribution of Maundy Money. Difficult to define. But there is virtue in it. Does it make sense to suggest that attending public readings is somehow for audiences an act of piety? To gods who are only a folk-memory. Maypoles. Morris Dancers. With writers possessed of some vague national/cultural King's Evil in which nobody *really* believes but . . . ?

John Hollingshead concluded his essay "Charles Dickens as a Reader" as follows:

Mr. Dickens scarcely knows the force of the engine which he holds in his hands — has scarcely mastered the scope and destination of his great design. He is now delighting elegant wearers of opera-cloaks and carriers of bouquets, dangling loungers who come to satisfy an idle curiosity; and stout well-to-do middle-class citizens, who have been blessed with the taught ability to read and write. Descend a little lower in the social scale, and we come upon a land containing thousands — nay, millions — who are only to be reached through their eyes and ears; to whom a printed book is a black, blurred, mysterious mass, notwithstanding many Acts of Parliament, educational commissions, and school-houses remarkable for their imposing style of architecture. Yet these people are men and women with hearts and souls — people willing to be taught, if they can be taught easily (for at forty, in the intervals of heavy labour, it is a sore task even to learn to read) — people ready to pay for being taught — people who know little, and never will know much, of moral principles, and who can only be reached and improved through their emotional sympathies.

Here is a wide and fruitful field for Mr. Dickens to cultivate, and in such a cause they gain a dignity who descend.

Hmmm!
Yes.
But that was before TV.